POINT HOPE
AN
ESKIMO VILLAGE
IN TRANSITION

THE AMERICAN
ETHNOLOGICAL SOCIETY
VIOLA E. GARFIELD
EDITOR

POINT HOPE

* * * AN

ESKIMO VILLAGE

IN TRANSITION

BY JAMES W. VANSTONE

SEATTLE · UNIVERSITY OF WASHINGTON PRESS

1962

For my

Mother and Father

ACKNOWLEDGMENTS

The field work on which this study is based was initiated and financed by the Arctic Aeromedical Laboratory at Ladd Air Force Base, Alaska, under contract number AF 41 (657)-32, project number 7-7957-4, and by the University of Alaska. The writer is grateful to personnel of the Aeromedical Laboratory for their assistance and encouragement, and to Dr. Wendell H. Oswalt who was associated with him in carrying out the project.

While at Point Hope, the writer enjoyed the hospitality and assistance of Mr. and Mrs. Charles J. Evans, the Bureau of Indian Affairs teachers, and the Rev. and Mrs. Rowland J. Cox of St. Thomas' Mission. Without their friendly interest and encouragement, life in the village would have been far less pleasant than it was.

Whatever merit there is to this study of Point Hope is due to the Point Hopers themselves. Since the writer relied heavily on participation and observation, nearly every individual in the community helped him to achieve a greater knowledge and understanding of community life. The following persons were particularly helpful because of close friendship with the writer: Mr. and Mrs. David Frankson, Mr. and Mrs. Daniel Lisbourne, Mr. and Mrs. William Lisbourne, Mr. and Mrs. Bernard Nash, Mr. and Mrs. Bob Tuckfield, Mr. and Mrs. Billy Weber, Mr. John Oktollik, Mr. Augustus Kowunna, and Mr. Luke Koonook.

Dr. Froelich Rainey, whose published reconstruction of Point Hope culture as it was prior to 1900 was of great value in the preparation of the present study, kindly allowed the writer to use his unpublished field notes.

Photographs were taken by the writer and Mrs. Rowland J. Cox. The maps and line drawings are the work of Mr. Wilbur Libby, Mr. William Berry, and the writer. Help and criticism in the

preparation of the manuscript has been given by Dr. Margaret
Lantis, Dr. Wendell H. Oswalt, the Reverend and Mrs. Rowland
J. Cox, Mrs. Gloria Bodner, and Mrs. Ernest Wolff. Dr. Verne
F. Ray, former American Ethnological Society editor, gave more
than usual attention to the preparation of the manuscript for publication. He assisted the author in the rephrasing of numerous portions of the book.

James W. VanStone

Toronto, Canada

CONTENTS

ILLUSTRATIONS

POINT HOPE

AN

ESKIMO VILLAGE

IN TRANSITION

INTRODUCTION

DURING the 1920's and 1930's when significant contributions were being made to the ethnology and archaeology of the eastern Eskimo area, anthropological research was just beginning in Alaska and was confined mostly to archaeological excavations in northwest Alaska where the large size of the prehistoric settlements, the richness of the material culture, and the excellence of the preservation due to frozen ground made the work particularly rewarding. For these reasons, and because of the geographical position of northern Alaska as the probable route of movements of peoples into the New World, this region has proved most attractive to archaeologists.

Until recently very little attention has been paid to the existing cultures of the people who inhabit this vast area. As late as 1940 the only comprehensive ethnographic studies of the Alaskan Eskimos were three monographs of the late nineteenth century dealing almost exclusively with material culture: *The Eskimo about Bering Strait* by E. W. Nelson (1899); *Ethnological Results of the Point Barrow Expedition* by J. Murdoch (1892); *Ethnographic Sketch of the Natives of Point Barrow* by P. H. Ray (1885). Important ethnographic data were also gathered by census enumerators in 1880 (U. S. Census Bureau, 1884) and 1890 (U. S. Census Bureau, 1893).

In 1947 Rainey published his reconstruction of the annual cycle of subsistence activities at Point Hope prior to 1900, and he and Larsen also published a generalized account of the annual cycle of the river people of northwest Alaska. The latter report is enhanced by an interesting reconstruction of the probable relations between inland and coastal economies at the beginning of the historic period (Larsen and Rainey, 1948, pp. 25-36).

In 1946 Lantis published two sections of a projected four-part study of the Eskimos of Nunivak Island in which the annual cycle is defined but the emphasis is on nonmaterial culture and mythology (Lantis, 1946). *Eskimo Childhood and Interpersonal Relationships: Bibliographies and Genealogies of the Nunivak Eskimo,* by Lantis, appeared in 1960. A monograph by Giddings dealing with his archaeological excavations along the Kobuk River contains considerable ethnographic information, mostly derived from historical sources, and he has also written a semipopular account of Kobuk River life (Giddings, 1952a, 1956). An ethnography of the Chugach Eskimos of southwestern Alaska (Birket-Smith, 1953), and a study of the Eskimo of Point Barrow and vicinity (Spencer, 1959) complete the reports dealing with the nonarchaeological aspects of Alaskan Eskimo culture published by trained anthropologists in recent years. These studies are largely devoted to the Eskimos before contact with Europeans. Relatively little attention has been given to the contemporary Alaskan Eskimo and his adjustments.

Contact between the western Alaskan Eskimos and European explorers, traders, and missionaries has taken place over a span of nearly 200 years, the contacts becoming increasingly more intensive during the period following World War II when military interests found Alaska to be important for defense purposes. Anthropologists working in the area in recent years have shown an interest in problems of culture change. As a result, there have been a few summaries of contact effects, particularly by Dr. Margaret Lantis whose field experience amply qualifies her to comment upon contemporary Alaskan Eskimo culture (Lantis, 1952, 1954, 1960); and a monograph on the contemporary culture of Gambell, a village on St. Lawrence Island (Hughes, 1960).

In the present study the major concern is with the functioning of a contemporary Eskimo community of western Alaska. Historical materials are utilized to provide a background but the study is functional and acculturational rather than historical.

Why should such a study be made? What enlightenment can it offer in our search for the basic mechanisms of culture? In the planning of the research at Point Hope the large questions gave rise to the formulation of many smaller and more specific queries, e. g., "Has the continued importance of basic subsistence activities in this community acted as a stabilizing influence on village life?" Such questions, in considerable number, served as the initial guidelines for the field research and provided a theoretical framework.

These preresearch formulations, i. e., those which survived, are not presented here, but, rather, in the concluding chapter, along with the actual findings.

The general character of the proposed study dictated that I should choose one of the villages on the coast north of Kotzebue Sound. There are five such villages. From south to north they are Kivalina, Point Hope, Point Lay, Wainwright, and Point Barrow. Kivalina and Point Lay are relatively small and have not been very stable in population over the last twenty or thirty years. In addition, Point Lay is also the site of extensive military construction. Point Barrow is a relatively cosmopolitan trading center with a sizable white population. Point Hope and Wainwright are roughly the same size and either village might have served the purposes of this inquiry. Point Hope was chosen because of certain advantages. An earlier ethnographic study by Rainey (1947) provided some readily available data. Also, Point Hope is a locality that has been continuously occupied for many hundreds of years and the population has remained stable for fifty years or more. Outside contacts in the form of military personnel or construction workers have been slight. It is a community without extremes of wealth or poverty. More than any other village on the northwest coast of Alaska, it is a closely knit community with strong community spirit, hence ideal for the purposes of the study.

I arrived at Point Hope on September 7, 1955, and left on August 20, 1956. Upon arrival I settled down as unobtrusively as possible in a rented house which I was able to get because it had been vacant for four years. From the first day I received many visitors in my home. Some were merely curious as to why I had come to live in the village; some wished to inquire about friends in Fairbanks.

With the exception of missionaries and schoolteachers, few white men have resided in Point Hope for any length of time. However the village is visited from time to time by representatives of the Bureau of Indian Affairs, the Alaska Department of Health, the National Guard, the Arctic Aeromedical Laboratory, and many other organizations; hence the villagers are only moderately curious when a new person arrives. Many associated me with the military because several years earlier an army observer had been stationed in the village for nearly two years. I explained the reasons for my presence and it was not long before I ceased to be regarded as a curiosity.

During the first few weeks considerable time was spent in the village store since it is a favorite gathering place. Home visits were exchanged and much information was obtained over a cup of coffee. During the early weeks of the study I worked for the Episcopal mission, which was hiring men to help repair one of its buildings. Being on the job eight hours a day with a crew of ap-

proximately fifteen men helped me to extend the circle of my ac-
quaintances.

Very little use was made of paid informants, the major reliance
being on participant observation. Gaps in my observations were
the bases for questioning, which was done informally while visiting
or entertaining. Occasionally, however, I found it advisable to
hire an informant to obtain such knowledge as the description of
ceremonies and the kinship terminology. Once friendships had
been established with a variety of individuals in the village, it was
not difficult to find opportunities to talk over village activities or
the behavior of people. The long night watches during the whaling
season were particularly satisfactory for these discussions. My
most profitable contacts were with men who belonged roughly to
my own age group, between twenty-five and forty.

The information obtained during the day was recorded in outline
form in a small notebook. At convenient times this was transferred
to five- by eight-inch punch cards that were punched for the major
categories of culture (i. e., the individual, social structure, work
round, and so on) as well as the subcategories (i. e., nuclear family, childhood, artifacts, hunting and fishing techniques). The
punched cards were filed according to an outline of desired data
that made it possible, throughout the course of the field work, to
determine what remaining aspects of culture needed to be covered
in order to give a representative picture of village life.

2

THE SETTING

THE POINT HOPE peninsula is the westernmost extension of the North American continent north of Bering Strait and lies approximately 125 miles north of the Arctic Circle (see Maps 1, 2). It resembles a triangular-shaped breakwater and consists of two bars that converge approximately fifteen miles west of the mainland and enclose a large body of shallow water known as Marryatt Inlet. The inlet opens to the sea through a narrow pass located north of the Kukpuk River. The gravel bar that forms the southern leg of the triangle extends southeast until it meets the rocky headlands of Cape Thompson. Six to ten miles from the top of the peninsula in this direction are located a series of shallow fresh-water lakes that are separated from the sea in some places by less than 200 feet of gravel beach. The northern leg of the triangle extends northwestward to the mainland where it merges with the lower reaches of the Lisburne Hills.

The peninsula has an area of approximately eighty square miles and consists of alluvial plains and marine beaches. The southern part of the peninsula is entirely a beach deposit composed of coarse sand and gravel, while the northern area comprises both marine beach and alluvial deposit. The unusual structure of the peninsula has been caused by the combined effects of ocean currents, pressure from the ice pack, and deposition from the Kukpuk River. The sea current flowing in a northerly direction through Bering Strait is deflected to the west of the steep, rocky shore at Cape Thompson and thus passes close to the shore at the western tip of the Point Hope peninsula.

The entire western end of the peninsula consists of a series of regular depressions separating parallel ridges that run in an east-west direction. The depressions vary from two to six feet in depth and some retain the water from melting snow throughout the en-

Map 1. Map of Alaska (showing locations mentioned in the text)

tire summer. It has been suggested that these ridges were formed
by the action of ice and current (Rainey, 1947, p. 19). At the present time the spit is in the process of building on the south side and
being cut away on the north. These changes are so rapid as to be
clearly noticeable over a relatively short period of years. Dr.
John Driggs, first missionary at Point Hope, estimated that the
north shore was cut back at least 185 feet during the eighteen years
of his residence in the area (Kindle, 1909, p. 108; much of the
material in this section is taken from Kindle, and Collier, 1906).

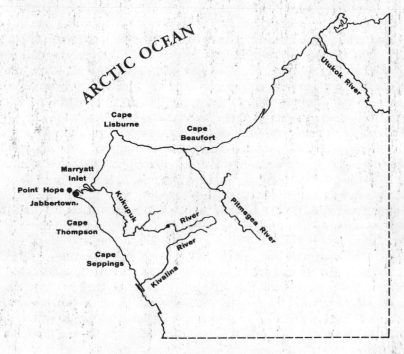

Map 2. Point Hope and vicinity

All of the peninsula that is made up of alluvial deposits is covered
by a typical tundra growth consisting of mosses, lichens, grasses,
and low flowering plants. The gravel beach area on the southern
side of the peninsula is bare of vegetation except for a sparse covering of grass. The vegetation is particularly thick in the low depressions where water stands during part of the summer months.

The elevation of the spit that forms the westernmost tip of the
peninsula does not exceed six feet above sea level, and the sea has
been known to wash over this area during exceptionally violent fall
storms.

The climate of the Point Hope peninsula is characterized by strong winds, but winter temperatures are not severe as compared with those in interior Alaska. Climatic records, kept sporadically at Point Hope village between 1888 and 1904, show that the lowest recorded temperature was -48° F. in February, 1892; the highest, 97° F. in July of 1897. Such high temperatures are very rare. During the summer of 1956, the temperature varied between 45° and 55° F. but cold northeast winds made it necessary to be warmly dressed at all times. During the winter of the same year, the temperature rarely fell below -30° F., but was frequently accompanied by winds from thirty to seventy-five miles per hour.

The area in the immediate vicinity of the Point Hope peninsula supports a considerable and varied fauna. The land holds great numbers of caribou as well as arctic wolves, foxes, brown and grizzly bears, ground squirrels, and various kinds of small rodents. Fish are not abundant today, but salmon, salmon trout, whitefish, and grayling are occasionally taken. Waterfowl of several varieties pass over the peninsula each spring and nest in the sea cliffs at Cape Lisburne and Cape Thompson. Sea mammals are essential to the economy of the Point Hope Eskimo and small hair seals, large bearded seals, walrus, belugas, and baleen whales are taken in great numbers every year in the sea off the Point Hope spit. Polar bears, which follow the pack ice hunting sea mammals, are also plentiful in the area.

On the western tip of the peninsula is located the village of Point Hope. The Eskimo name for the village and the tip of the peninsula is *Tikeraq* (index finger). On some maps, the peninsula itself is labeled Point Hope, and the village, Tigara. A barren, low, isolated, and windswept point seems a strange location for one of the largest Eskimo villages in Alaska, but the excellence of the sea mammal hunting has made it a favored place for human habitation for many centuries.

On the northwest tip of the peninsula are the remains of a large abandoned village which is referred to as the Old Tigara site by archaeologists (Larsen and Rainey, 1948). The old houses and midden refuse are scattered along two grass covered ridges. The modern village is simply an extension of the Old Tigara site, with the houses constructed in rows along the ridges just as they were in prehistoric times.

From the air, the village appears as two long rows of houses running east and west and separated by a narrow slough (Map 3). Closer examination shows that the houses have been built along the parallel ridges that are the characteristic feature of the end of the

peninsula. The village consists of some fifty houses, all of which
are of frame construction although there are a few that closely
approximate old, semisubterranean type. These old houses are
located at the west end of the village nearest the abandoned section. The village has grown from west to east; families who have
built new houses in recent years have built them at the eastern end
of the two rows. Many of the frame houses have a covering of sod
around them so that they give the appearance of old-style houses.

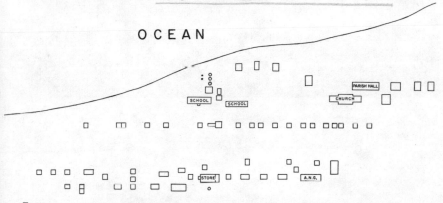

Map 3. Plan of the village of Point Hope, 1956

The village is dominated architecturally by a number of large
buildings that are the location of many community functions. Cen-
trally located behind the northern row of dwellings are the school
buildings, consisting of two frame classroom structures with resi-
dences attached. The newer of these buildings was completed during the summer of 1955. Point Hope, with a population of approximately 265 in 1956, including 67 school children, has had a two-
teacher school for many years although it is supposed to have three
teachers. The new classroom and residence is intended for a third
teacher. Included in the complex of school buildings are a work-
shop, cold storage for ice in winter, and a small building housing
the electric light plants.

At the northeast end of the village are located the buildings of
St. Thomas' Mission of the Protestant Episcopal Church, the only
church in Point Hope. These buildings were moved from their
former location one mile northeast of the village during the fall
of 1955. In addition to a church building, there are a large parish
hall, the missionary's residence, and three storage buildings, one
of which was originally intended as a hospital but was never used
for that purpose.

In the southeast corner of the village is located the Alaska Na-

Plate I-A. Public Buildings

The school buildings

The village store

Plate I-B. Public Buildings

The church and parish hall

Alaska National Guard building

tional Guard building, a drill hall for the local National Guard unit, which is occasionally used for other public events.

The village store, affiliated with the Alaska Native Industries Cooperative Association, is a large frame establishment with metal sheathing on the outside. Inside, it is very much like a country store in appearance and is the gathering and visiting place for many villagers. Attached to the store is a residence for the store manager and his family, and there are two storage buildings located in the immediate vicinity. The store also owns a residence, a converted Quonset, which is intended for the assistant store manager but in 1956 was rented to a widow and her family.

Less than thirty years ago, the store, school, and mission buildings were the only frame structures in the village. Today, when all the villagers occupy frame dwellings, they still stand out as the largest and most distinctive buildings in Point Hope.

According to an executive order of July 8, 1930, approximately ten square miles of the Point Hope village area, including all the present village, is reserved for educational purposes and the use of the resident population. This order prohibits commercial activities by white men in the area except with the permission of the Secretary of the Interior. This ruling has been invoked several times in the past to prohibit traders in Kotzebue from opening branch stores in the village.

Point Hope is located approximately 175 miles from Kotzebue, and twenty-five years ago was considered to be extremely isolated and seldom visited by outsiders except during the summer months when the sea was open and ships could anchor off the point. With the advent of scheduled air transportation, however, the picture changed completely, and the village is now easily accessible at all times of the year. Formerly, a trip by dog team to Kotzebue was three hard days' travel with a day of rest somewhere along the line. Today, the trip can be made by airplane in approximately one and one-half hours.

In 1956 Point Hope was served by a local airline which made three trips a week from Kotzebue, stopping at Noatak and Kivalina, and continuing on to the military base at Cape Lisburne before returning to Kotzebue. The airline possessed a variety of single-engine equipment and the aircraft used depended upon the amount of freight, mail, and passengers. The fare from Kotzebue to Point Hope was $38.50 including tax, with a 10 per cent reduction for round trips. The fare for a trip of comparable distance in the United States would be approximately $9.00. Since 1956 an air-

strip has been constructed and larger airplanes can now land at
the village.

The village is also served once a year by the Bureau of Indian
Affairs' ship *North Star*, which brings supplies from Seattle for
all Alaskan coastal villages having stores affiliated with the Alaska
Native Industries Cooperative Association. In addition, a transport
company in Kotzebue makes irregular trips to Point Hope during
the summer with freight. Usually they do not stop at the village
unless there is a large order to be unloaded, such as drums of oil
for the mission; it is a negligible transportation resource as far
as the villagers are concerned. However, the store occasionally
orders merchandise to be delivered by this means if they are out
of a heavy, fast-selling item that cannot profitably be brought in
by air.

The village of Kotzebue, located at the tip of Baldwin Peninsula
in the Kotzebue Sound region, is a cosmopolitan Eskimo village
with a considerable white population. It can be said to be the trading center for the whole Kotzebue Sound region and for as far north
as Point Hope. The villages north of Point Hope are in the sphere
of influence of Point Barrow, partly because they are served by
airplanes flying out of that village. At Kotzebue is located a Bureau
of Indian Affairs' hospital and dental clinic. There is in residence
at the hospital a doctor who maintains daily contact with the villages by means of a radio schedule. Some Point Hopers order supplies from the traders at Kotzebue, but since the goods must be
shipped in by air it is very expensive and the means is resorted
to only in case of particular shortages. In the summer of 1955,
when the local store was out of canned milk, some families ordered milk for their infants to be sent from Kotzebue by airplane.

Point Hope has had a post office since early in the century, but
as recently as 1939 there were only five regular mail deliveries
a year; in November and January by dog team, in March and April
by air, and in July by boat. Occasionally other aircraft and boats
coming to the village brought mail. In 1956 mail was received on
every airplane and the amount of business transacted at the post
office had increased to the point where over $100 worth of stamps
were sold every month. The increase in air service has brought
about a marked rise in the use of mail-order services, which in
turn has boosted the business of the post office.

Today the village of Point Hope is far from being isolated. Every
airplane arrival brings news and products from the outside. Radio
contact makes medical care much more efficient and only a few

hours away. However, when mechanical difficulties render the radio inoperative and inclement weather makes it impossible for airplanes to fly, the isolation of the village is complete.

3

HISTORICAL BACKGROUND

IN ADDITION to being the site of a large village today, the Point Hope area has long been known to contain some of the most extensive archaeological sites to be found anywhere in the Arctic. The Old Tigara site, located west of the present village, is one of the largest middens in northwest Alaska. When visiting Point Hope in 1924, Knud Rasmussen counted 122 houses in the old site (Rasmussen, 1927, p. 329), while Rainey estimated that there were about seventy still remaining when he began excavations during the summer of 1939 (Rainey, 1947, p. 20). The fact that there were only about forty remaining in 1956 indicates the rapidity with which the north side of the spit is being cut away by the sea and ice.

The now famous Ipiutak site is located at the western end of Marryatt Inlet and represents a culture that seems to be basically Eskimo but from which whaling equipment, an important aspect of late prehistoric, and modern Eskimo life in the area, is absent. Estimates of the age of the Ipiutak site, based on carbon-14 dates, suggest that it is approximately 1,000 years old.

The presence of these extensive archaeological sites indicates that Point Hope is one of the longest continuously occupied village sites in Alaska. Perhaps for this reason, the people seem to possess a sense of cohesiveness as a village. Although continuity of population cannot be proved, Point Hopers nevertheless consider themselves tied together as members of a community with roots in one place for a long time. This feeling of community membership does not seem to be present in neighboring villages like Kivalina, Kotzebue, and Point Lay, which were established relatively recently and consist of groups of families who moved there from somewhere else.

The archaeological remains in the Point Hope area suggest a population much larger than any recorded in recent times. The

Ipiutak site alone contained over 500 houses when Larsen and Rainey discovered it in 1939 (Larsen and Rainey, 1948, p. 16) and many more had doubtless been cut away by the encroaching sea and ice. Although there is considerable doubt as to whether all these houses were occupied at the same time, it does seem that the population at Point Hope was once considerably larger than it is today. Diseases introduced from American whaling vessels after 1850 were doubtless partly responsible for the decline.

The earliest recorded census figures for the village indicate a population that has remained stable down to the present. The enumerator of the tenth census records 276 persons as living at Point Hope in 1880 (U.S. Census Bureau, 1884, p. 4) and ten years later there were 295 (U.S. Census Bureau, 1893, p. 8). In 1908, Dr. John Driggs noted that there were 168 people in the village living in 25 households, while 44 people were living at Beacon Hill in 14 households and 48 at Jabbertown in 10 households (St. Thomas' Mission records). Both these communities, now abandoned, were located southeast of Point Hope along the southern shore of the peninsula. In the eighteen-year period between 1937 and 1955 the population varied by no more than 40 individuals. It should be kept in mind that census figures, even under the most favorable circumstances, are accurate for only a short time after they are recorded, as people are constantly leaving or entering the village for one reason or another. This was probably more true thirty or forty years ago, when trapping and commercial whaling often took people away from the village for long periods of time.

Although the people of Point Hope have always considered the village to be their permanent home, in the past their hunting, fishing, and trapping activities have encompassed a much wider territory. Within the memory of living old people, family groups hunted and fished as far north as the Utukok River and as far south as the Kivalina River. Caribou hunting parties traveled inland along the Utukok, and fishing and caribou hunting was particularly good near the headwaters of the Pitmagea River. South of Cape Seppings and inland along the Kivalina River was also good caribou hunting territory, while the lower reach of the Kukpuk River was frequented for fall fishing just as it is today. Point Hope people, therefore, were thoroughly familiar with the coastal area from the mouth of the Utukok south to the mouth of the Kivalina, as well as a considerable distance inland along the whole area. The mouth of the Utukok was the site of a summer trading rendezvous and a similar center was located to the south near the present village of Kotzebue (see Map 2, p. 9).

An observer near the end of the nineteenth century reports that the Point Hopers claimed they once exercised control over all the country from Kotzebue Sound north to Icy Cape, and eastward as far as Deviation Peak which is slightly northwest of Kiana on the Kobuk River. In the latter part of the eighteenth century, the people from around Noatak began encroaching on Point Hope territory and it was not long until they occupied the southern part of the Point Hope domain as far north as Kivalina. One summer, about the year 1800, a great land and sea fight reportedly took place between Point Hope and Noatak Eskimos just below Cape Seppings. The Point Hope people were defeated and forced to withdraw from all that part of the country. So badly were they defeated that they lost most of their good hunters and suffered greatly from famine (Wells, 1890, pp. 10-11). Wars of this kind have taken on an almost legendary character in the minds of the Point Hopers, but there can be no doubt that such battles did actually take place.

It seems certain that the people of Point Hope either controlled or were familiar with a large area in all directions from the village. In the days when fur prices were high and trapping was an important part of the economy, families built cabins in certain recognized areas and did their trapping there, returning year after year. Many families stayed away from the village for the entire winter, returning only for whaling in the spring. With the decline in fur prices trapping ceased to be important, and this together with the presence of a school and church at Point Hope has tended to keep the people close to the village. With the exception of fall fishing up the Kukpuk River, hunting and fishing trips along the coast and into the interior are seldom of more than a few days' duration.

It has been nearly 300 years since the people of Point Hope first became aware of the white man. European trade goods from a trading post established by the Russians at Anadyr in 1648 probably reached Point Hope before the beginning of the eighteenth century, or at least 125 years before any white man saw the village.

Point Hope was observed and named by Captain F. W. Beechey, Commander of H. M. S. *Blossom* in August of 1826, when he passed through Bering Strait to cruise northward along the northwest coast of Alaska in cooperation with the second Franklin expedition. Captain Cook must have passed close to the village in 1778, but, situated as it is on a low gravel beach, it is not visible any distance at sea. Beechey's men first became aware of the Point Hope peninsula when "We ascended Cape Thompson and discovered low land jutting out from the coast to the W. N. W. as far as the eye could reach. As this point had never been placed on our charts, I named it Point Hope in compliment to Sir William Johnstone Hope" (Beechey, 1831, I, 362). Of the village itself, Beechey says: "On nearing it we perceived a forest of stakes driven into the ground for the purpose of keeping the property of the natives off the ground, and beneath them several round hillocks, which we afterwards found to be the Esquimaux yourts, or underground winter habitations" (Beechey, 1831, I, 363).

In September of the following year, Lieutenant Belcher, in command of the barge from the *Blossom,* was forced ashore at Point Hope by bad weather. He had been detailed to look for signs of Franklin and to explore the cove north of the Point Hope spit which Beechey named Marryatt Cove. On most maps today it is referred to as an inlet rather than a cove. Shortly after leaving Point Hope, the *Blossom's* barge was wrecked and several men were lost (Beechey, 1831, II, 277).

The search for Franklin's third expedition resulted in a considerable amount of Arctic exploration, much of it carried out by the British. Between 1848 and 1854 most of the coastal villages between Port Clarence and Point Barrow were visited by the search ships. The Russians felt that they had done insufficient exploration in northern Alaska, and during the summer of 1838 sent an expedition under the command of Lieutenant Kashevarov in the brig *Polifem* to explore the northern coast line, particularly the area east of Point Barrow. This expedition must have passed by Point Hope but Kashevarov makes no mention of it. Later he experienced considerable trouble with the people at Point Barrow and was forced to return before he made any explorations to the east (Tikhmenev, 1863, Part I, p. 338).

Although Point Hope was first visited by Europeans in 1826, it was at least another twenty-five years before the people of the village had any direct contact with the outside world. In the early years of the nineteenth century the whaling industry confined its activities almost exclusively to the Atlantic and southern Pacific oceans, but in 1838 the great northwest whaling grounds were discovered and five years later whales were first taken along the coast of Kamchatka and in the Okhotsk Sea. Ten years later, in 1848, a vessel from Sag Harbor, N. Y. made a very successful voyage in the Arctic Ocean north of Bering Strait. This was the beginning of whaling in the Arctic and the fleet frequenting the Arctic grounds increased rapidly in numbers with each passing year (Tower, 1907, pp. 59-60).

The people of Point Hope and other north Alaskan villages at first thought the whalers to be stupid because they did not understand the Eskimo language. Later there were hard feelings between the two groups and the Eskimos are known to have attacked parties of whalemen who came ashore to fill water casks or to gather driftwood for fuel.

The whaling ships came into the Arctic mainly for the purpose of obtaining baleen, the long flexible strips in a bowhead whale's mouth, which serve to strain the great animal's food from the water. Baleen was used for a variety of manufactured articles such as buttons and corset stays. The value of baleen in 1850, when vessels first started going into the Arctic Ocean, was a little more than 32 cents a pound. By 1880 it was worth $2.00 a pound and in 1905, $4.90 a pound (Tower, 1907, p. 128). Since each whale contains several hundred pounds of this valuable material, it is not surprising that the animal was eagerly sought after and that the fleet grew rapidly. Great quantities of whale oil were also collected to be rendered for soap, candles, and other products.

The steam whaling vessel was introduced into the Arctic fleet in 1880 and brought considerable changes to Arctic whaling. Up to this time the northern fleet had been accustomed to winter in San Francisco or at some other port in the Pacific. As soon as spring arrived, the ships went north again to wait for the ice to break up so that they could pass through Bering Strait. With the introduction of the steam whaling vessel, however, it was possible for the ships to remain in the Arctic during the winter in order to be earlier on the grounds when the ice broke up in the spring. By 1893, one fourth of the vessels whaling in the north Pacific and Arctic oceans wintered off the mouth of the Mackenzie River. Another group of ships wintered in the vicinity of Point Barrow, and some at Herschel Island. A tender visited the ships to carry supplies and to receive any oil or baleen that had been taken (Tower, 1907, pp. 62-65).

The pursuit of whales in the Arctic was at times extremely dangerous. Often the ice would close in upon vessels that were short on provisions and much suffering and hardship would be caused the whalemen through the long, hard winters. In September of 1897, approximately 275 men were marooned at Point Barrow and remained there until August, 1898. An overland expedition in charge of personnel from the U. S. Revenue Cutter *Bear* drove reindeer from Teller to Point Barrow for their relief (*Report of the Cruise of the* Bear, 1899, p. 102). Vessels were occasionally wrecked and their crews forced to make the best of it in an inhospitable environment. In October of 1880, the bark *Small Ohio* was wrecked

off the edge of the Point Hope spit and most of the crew were lost.
A few survived and lived with the Eskimos until they were picked
up the following summer (Cook, 1926, p. 34).

Beginning in 1880, a United States revenue cutter cruised in the
Arctic Ocean every summer to protect the whaling interests of the
United States and particularly to prevent the illicit sale of liquor
to the Eskimos. They were also supposed to enforce the law pro-
hibiting the sale of breech-loading arms and ammunition. This
law was a source of handicap to the Eskimos, as many of them had
purchased their rifles previous to the enactment of the law and
found that they were unable to obtain ammunition for them. This
was particularly difficult because they had lost their proficiency
with their old types of weapons and had come to depend upon the
rifle. In spite of the efforts of the revenue cutters, the Eskimos
were able to carry on a flourishing trade for guns, cartridges, and
liquor with the whalers who were prepared to give anything in exchange for quantities of baleen (Hooper, 1881, p. 45).

The arrival of the whaling fleet every spring was greatly antici-
pated by the people of Point Hope and other north Alaskan coastal
villages. Point Hope was the first place that the whalemen touched
after recruiting at Port Clarence, and they usually employed some
local men to help man the ships as they worked their way north
(U.S. Census Bureau, 1893, p. 137). The whaling ships were always plagued with desertions among their crews, and this was particularly true during the last few years of the nineteenth century
when men were looking for a free trip to Alaska in order to get to
the gold fields. Deserters from whaling ships were often forced to
spend the winter in Eskimo villages and the earliest close contacts
with white men at Point Hope came about in this manner.

Captain M. A. Healy, of the Revenue Marine Steamer *Corwin* that
cruised in the Arctic Ocean during the summer of 1884, reported
that the people of Point Hope had great quantities of baleen saved
up to trade with the whalers and they would trade only for whisky.
Since whaling boats were constantly passing and repassing Point
Hope, he deemed it necessary to station some men there during
the summer of 1884 to prevent trading with the people for liquor.
Many whaling captains boasted to Healy of bringing a great deal of
liquor into the Arctic to trade but dumping it overboard when they
learned that there was a revenue cutter in the area (Healy, 1889,
p. 11).

During the 1880's it became the policy for individuals and firms
to establish whaling stations at various points along the Arctic
coast and to conduct whaling from shore, shipping the baleen to

the states. There were, during the winter of 1897-98, thirteen
such stations strung out at intervals along the shore between Point
Hope and Cape Seppings, owned and run by white men. These outfits needed, besides the white employees, many Eskimos to help
man the boats during the whaling season. The Eskimos were paid
by the month in such items as flour, crackers, black tobacco,
matches, lead, rifles, ammunition, and molasses *(Cruise of the
Bear,* 1899, p. 25).

Such a station was established at Point Hope during the summer
of 1887 by a San Francisco firm. At that time, the people of the
village were being terrorized by a local strong man, Attungoruk,
who had made himself a kind of chief of the village. Although at
first opposed to the presence of the whaling station, Attungoruk
later came to see its value and obtained control of a large supply of
trade goods from the whaling captains. It was this more than anything else that enhanced his prestige in the village and he became a
spokesman for the Eskimos in their dealings with the whalers.
Gradually he began to assume dictatorial powers and his eventual
loss of prestige seems to have been due to the fact that he began
taking other men's wives by force. Finally, having angered the
other men in the village and incurred the enmity of relatives of
people he had harmed, he was shot to death on February 14, 1889,
as he slept among his several wives (Rainey, 1947, p. 243; Wells,
1890, pp. 10-11). It is said that the relations between the village
and the whaling station were much more peaceful after the death
of Attungoruk.

The various whaling stations established in the vicinity of Point
Hope needed many more men than were locally available to help
run their boats during the whaling season. As a result, large numbers of Eskimos came up the coast from the region around Kotzebue
Sound and the Noatak and Kobuk rivers to work for the stations. A
large population would gather each spring about six miles east of
Point Hope, at a location that came to be called Jabbertown because of the many different Eskimo dialects spoken there along
with the additional languages of the crews of whaling vessels. When
whaling ended, the people returned to their own villages and Jabbertown was deserted, except for the whaling stations, until the
following spring.

Whaling continued to be a profitable activity in the Arctic through
the last decade of the nineteenth century and the beginning of the
twentieth. Representative importations of baleen at San Francisco
for those years show that the whaling ships were extremely successful (Tower, 1907, p. 130).

1885	441,400 lb.	1901	76,550 lb.
1887	561,694 lb.	1904	102,000 lb.
1889	291,400 lb.	1905	38,200 lb.

In 1887 the whaling fleet consisted of thirty-two vessels (Aldrich, 1889, p. 137), but by 1912 there were only two companies operating in the north with but five vessels (Rabot, 1914, p. 485). The introduction of new materials to replace baleen resulted in a sharp drop in the price. This, together with a marked depletion of the whale population, made it impossible to continue whaling on a large scale. By 1915, whaling in the Arctic Ocean had come to an end.

It was through intercourse with the whaling vessels that the people of Point Hope were first exposed to American culture, but the effect was largely detrimental as far as the village was concerned. The crews of the whaling vessels taught the people how to make intoxicating liquor and then took advantage of their desire to obtain the raw materials for its manufacture in trade for the valuable baleen. They introduced venereal and other diseases that had never prevailed in the area before and consequently caused a frightful mortality. Many northern villages lost fully half their population in a few years, while Point Hope lost 12 per cent of its population during the fall of 1902 alone when a small whaling schooner that had wintered near the mouth of the Mackenzie River landed some women from that area who had the measles (Driggs, 1903). It seems safe to say that the Eskimo population of northwest Alaska has never recovered numerically from the epidemics brought about by diseases introduced from the whaling ships.[1]

During the summer of 1889, the U.S.S. *Thetis* cruised in the Arctic Ocean to protect the whaling interests of the United States. In command was Lieutenant Commander Charles A. Stockton who was very much impressed with what he considered to be the desperate condition of the Eskimos along the northern coast. Upon his return to the United States, he wrote to Dr. Sheldon Jackson, who was then general agent for education in Alaska, and to the board of missions of the Episcopal Church. Dr. Jackson began negotiating with several Protestant missionary societies for the purpose of securing the simultaneous establishment of missions at Cape Prince of Wales, Point Hope, and Point Barrow. The Congregationalists were to go to Wales, the Episcopal Church to Point Hope, and the

---

[1]For a more detailed discussion of Arctic whaling, see Van Stone, 1958b.

Presbyterians to Point Barrow. In 1890, all three missions were officially established and the U.S. Revenue Cutter *Bear* transported the men selected to have charge of them. A schooner sailed from San Francisco with materials for the three schoolhouses that were to be a part of the missions, and the crew from the ship helped to erect the first buildings (Stuck, 1920, pp. 28, 33-34).

The first missionary to St. Thomas' Mission at Point Hope was Dr. John B. Driggs, a medical man from Wilmington, Delaware. He began work with a day school which opened in October of 1890, but did not begin to teach the Christian faith until he had had some success with the school and had established himself in the village. Dr. Driggs remained at Point Hope for eighteen years, and was replaced by the Rev. A. R. Hoare who held the position for twelve years and constructed the mission house in 1912. In 1920, Mr. Hoare was murdered by a young white man who was a teacher at the mission school (Goodman, 1940). Between the time of Mr. Hoare's death and the present there have been five priests in charge of St. Thomas' Mission; even so, there were some years in which there was no priest in residence. Additional buildings were constructed and the church enlarged. During Dr. Driggs's period of tenure he made trips by dog team to the neighboring villages of Kivalina and Point Lay, and these became outstations of the mission at Point Hope. St. Thomas' Mission is the second oldest mission of the Episcopal Church in Alaska, having been established three years after the founding of Christ Church Mission at Anvik.

During the winter of 1889, when the establishment of a mission at Point Hope was under consideration, the Bureau of Education entered into a contract with the Episcopal Church for the establishment of a school in the village. The Church at first received $2,000 a year to help run the school but this assistance was discontinued in 1894 (Lavrischeff, unpublished Ph.D. thesis).

During the summer of 1904, Mr. W. T. Lopp, superintendent of reindeer stations and schools in northwestern Alaska, made several trips to Point Hope and supervised the construction of a government school building at Jabbertown, where many village people lived at the time (Jackson, 1904, p. 113). Several years were required for the completion of this building and it was operated separately from the mission school. It was torn down and rebuilt at Point Hope sometime during the early 1920's. Meanwhile, the Episcopal Church continued to run a school in conjunction with the government until 1924, when it was handed over to the Bureau of Education. The Point Hope school, along with other village schools in Alaska, remained administratively under the Bureau of Education of the Department of the Interior until 1931, when control was transferred to the Bureau of Indian Affairs (Anderson and Eels, 1935, p. 215).

Domestic reindeer were brought into Alaska near the village of Teller on Seward Peninsula largely through the efforts of Dr. Sheldon Jackson and Captain Healy of the Revenue Cutter Service. A total of 171 deer were purchased in Siberia and brought to Alaska in 1892. Over the next ten years 1,280 deer were imported, and by 1930 the government supervising agency in charge of reindeer estimated that the herd had multiplied to over 600,000 animals (Anderson and Eels, 1935, p. 169). This estimate was based on the known increase rate of reindeer but without adequate account of losses.

Since the original importations of reindeer were supposed to be for the benefit of the Eskimo population, the Bureau of Education brought Chukchee herders from Siberia and later Lapp herders from northern Norway to teach the people the proper methods of caring for the herds. A system of apprenticeships for Eskimos was established, and as they became experienced in herding through working with the Lapp herders they became individual owners of deer. The Lapp families were also given a certain part of the herd increase in order to maintain their interest in the project (Hadwen and Palmer, 1922, p. 2).

In 1894, two men from Point Hope were sent to Teller to learn reindeer herding. One of these men, Eelectoona, took part of his herd and some government deer back to Point Hope in 1908. Most of the Point Hope herds originated at Kivalina and were under Kivalina supervision until about 1921, when they were moved north. The reindeer range in the Point Hope area was from Cape Beaufort to Cape Thompson and to the headwaters of the Pitmagea and Kukpuk rivers (Map 2, p. 9).

At first the reindeer did well at Point Hope. Most of the animals were individually owned and identified by special marks on the ears. However, this proved to be an unsatisfactory arrangement because the herds were hard to separate on the basis of individual marks. In March of 1926, all deer were counted into one herd owned by a joint stock company of Eskimos. When deer were butchered and sold the payment went to maintain the herd. In June of the same year a count showed 4,100 animals, and six years later there were over 6,000. The herd seems to have maintained its size until 1938, when the first sizable decrease was noted. In 1939-40 the herd numbered approximately 4,000 deer, but by 1945 there were only 500 and these were not being herded because of lack of interest on

the part of the people and the fact that other work was more profitable. In July of 1947 there were 327 deer and the herd was returned to the government because it was too small to pay its way.
A herder was hired, but when, in 1948, he left the deer to get supplies, the remaining 250 animals disappeared (Lantis, 1952a, p.
142).

The attempt to make reindeer herders out of the Alaskan Eskimos was largely unsuccessful for a variety of reasons. The deer
themselves were subject to various parasites and were killed in
large numbers by wolves. If not carefully watched by herdsmen,
they tended to wander off with the caribou. Certain areas were
overgrazed through careless herding. Most significant of all, perhaps, was the fact that the coastal Eskimos of northwest Alaska
are a sedentary people who follow a definite cycle of hunting and
fishing activities quite foreign to the nomadic routine of close-
herding. At Point Hope, for instance, even the most dedicated
herders desired to return to the village for the spring whaling activities, and it was at this time that large numbers of deer wan-
dered away and were lost. (Most of the material on reindeer herding was taken from reports in the Point Hope school files.)

*caribou herding
a failure because
not congruent with
seasonal cycle.*

4

THE SEASONAL CYCLE
OF SUBSISTENCE ACTIVITIES

Autumn

Toward the end of September or the first week in October, most of the Point Hope men who obtained summer employment away from the village have returned. Many of them like to be back by the time the Department of the Interior ship *North Star* makes its annual visit in mid-September, and the rest return shortly afterward. Much summer employment at various points along the Arctic coast and in Fairbanks now lasts well into the fall and early winter, but the Point Hope men, for the most part, prefer to return to the village in time for the fall hunting activities and preparation for winter.

Fishing for grayling at the mouth and along the lower reaches of the Kukpuk River is probably the most important fall activity. During the first week of October, boatloads of people leave the village for Kukpuk fish camps. It is about thirty miles from the village to the camps and often the skin boats, powered by outboard motors and loaded with camping gear, are pulled overland by dogs or the mission jeep to Marryatt Inlet, about a mile northeast of the village, where they are launched for the trip to the mouth of the river. In autumn the weather is often stormy and the boats seldom attempt to travel on the open ocean to the mouth of the Kukpuk. Even the inlet can become very rough if a strong north or south wind is blowing. The boats return after unloading at camp as freeze-up is near. Some people wait until after freeze-up and make the entire trip by dog team. Usually only the women and older men make the trip and they camp in extended family groups. Other members of the families make occasional trips by dog teams back and forth from the village to the fish camps, carrying supplies and returning with loads of fish. Not all the families go to the same place.

Some camp at the mouth of the river while others go upstream a short way. Some families have cabins at the various good fishing places and return there year after year; others move around from year to year.

There are three fishing methods used during the fall. If ice has not formed on the river, the fishing is done from shore with a pole, line, and lure. Sometimes stones are laid out in the water so that those who are fishing can walk farther out from shore. If the ice has formed, but is not too thick, nets are placed under the ice. The most common method, however, is to fish through holes in the ice with line and lure. A piece of polished ivory with hooks or a piece of colored cloth on a hook is used as a lure. The fish caught are simply allowed to freeze and are brought back to the village by the sackful.

In the fall of 1955, all families had returned to the village from fish camps by the fifteenth of November. This was a few weeks earlier than usual because the fishing was unusually poor. In a normal year, some families stay in camp until Thanksgiving and possibly somewhat later.

The hunting of caribou is also an important fall activity. These animals are hunted in the highlands of the interior, along the lower Kukpuk River, or along the coast to the north and south. Groups of hunters leave the village by outboard-motor-powered skin boat, enter Marryatt Inlet and go to the mouth of the Kukpuk River, up which they proceed until caribou are sighted. The caribou are killed with high-powered rifles and their meat provides a welcome change from the fish diet that predominates during the fall months.

Caribou-hunting groups are organized by owners of boats and owners of outboard motors—not always the same—who take members of their own or related families. When the hunters return from a successful hunt, the meat is laid out on the beach and divided equally among all those who made the trip, with the exception of the boat and motor owners who receive an additional full share. After the division is made, the meat is placed in separate piles and each hunter is responsible for removing his share to his home. The meat is eaten immediately as there is seldom enough to warrant storage. Caribou hunters are never away from the village for more than four or five days at a time and a hunter will seldom make more than one or two trips during the fall.

The southward movement of various migratory birds also provides a limited amount of food. Eiders and other ducks are hunted with shotguns as they fly over the spit or rest on the slough and small lakes near the village. Large numbers of snowy owls pass

by the Point Hope spit on their way south and are either shot with
small caliber rifles or trapped with small spring traps. Baited
traps are placed on projecting rocks, whale bones, and other high
places where owls land. Sea gulls and ptarmigan are also hunted.
The latter are not plentiful although a few are taken in the hills
behind Jabbertown. Sea gulls are eaten only in times of food shortage.

In addition to the hunting activities described above, the men
devote much time during the fall months in preparation for winter. Sleds are built or repaired and dog harnesses are made ready.
Houses are repaired and elaborate storm sheds and dog shelters
are constructed of oil drums and snow blocks. Many men cut and
pile snow blocks around the full perimeter of their houses in order
to insure greater protection from winter winds.

The hunting and fishing during the fall months is seldom more
than sufficient for immediate needs, and the people rely heavily
upon the seal and whale meat stored up in underground caches
from the previous spring. Each family has such a cache, dug into
the frozen debris of the Old Tigara site at the west end of the Point
Hope spit. If hunting had been poor the preceding spring, fall might
be a time of food shortage. Such shortages are sometimes offset
by purchases of food at the village store with money earned during
summer employment. Dog food in particular is short at this time
of year and dogs must get along on very little until winter seal
hunting begins. Some men make trips for many miles along the
beach in the hope of finding a dead walrus that has drifted ashore,
or other dead animals that can be utilized for dog food.

Under aboriginal conditions, the autumn season was the time
of numerous ceremonies in the ceremonial houses (dance or club
houses, termed *qalegis);* many of these were for the purpose of
bringing success in whaling (Rainey, 1947, pp. 245-53). Some of
these ceremonies survive today and are performed at Christmas
time. Formerly, when the first mush ice appeared off the point,
each *umelik* (whaling captain) hired a skilled craftsman to make
the wooden pot that his wife used to "give a drink to the whales
killed by his crew" (Rainey, 1947, p. 245). Today the appearance of
the first mush ice is observed by a feast, consisting of the whale's
tail, given for the whole village by those whaling captains who
killed a whale the preceding spring, but fewer than five during their
careers. A similar feast is given in the spring by those with more
than five whales to their credit. There was no fall feast in 1955
because the only whale killed the preceding spring was taken by a
captain with a record of more than five whales.

Winter

The winter seal hunting normally begins in late October or early November when the shore ice has formed and is solid enough for walking. When the ice extends only a short way out into the water, hunters move up and down the beach on foot or with dog teams, watching for hair seals or bearded seals to come up. Later, as the ice extends further out to sea, the hunter walks out on the new ice, testing it carefully as he goes. For this purpose he carries a long stick with an ice pick at one end to test the ice as he walks, and a hook at the other end for retrieving seals killed close to the edge of the ice. In the early winter when new ice is constantly being formed close to shore the hunters prefer not to take their dogs on the ice, but rather drag a small boat on a sled to retrieve seals that are shot too far from the edge. The small boat used for seal hunting in both winter and spring is pointed at both ends, seldom more than six or seven feet in length, and covered with a single bearded-seal skin. The frame is constructed of wood and the ribs of baleen. These little boats can be transported on a regular sled hauled by dogs, or on a small boat sled pulled by hand. They are extremely useful in hunting at large open leads where the seals cannot be retrieved directly from the ice.

Informants could remember no time when kayaks were used, nor were they able to remember under what circumstances this type of boat passed out of existence. One man mentioned that kayaks were too long to fit on a sled while the small skin boat was just the right size. Thus the kayak may have ceased to be used at the time dog teams were first used on the ice. Rainey's informants claimed that the erratic sea current that moves past Point Hope made the use of kayaks very dangerous. Several generations ago, some men hunted seals in kayaks before the pack ice returned; but they occasionally found that when the sea current suddenly decreased new ice formed between them and the shore, too thin to walk on but too thick to be broken through with a kayak. Many hunters are said to have been lost in this way (Rainey, 1947, p. 253).

During December, January, and February the pack ice moves in and the hunters must go far out to find open leads where seals and an occasional bearded seal may be shot. On cold, calm days there is very little open water and the hunters often gather on top of an especially high pressure-ridge and watch for open leads. The small leads are created by the slow movement of the ice and they freeze quickly. When all the surrounding leads have frozen, the hunters regather on the high ridges to look for new leads in other directions, at the same time watching for polar bears.

Breathing-hole hunting, characteristic of all coastal Eskimos, is not practiced to any great extent at Point Hope because it requires a long, tiresome wait and there is also a good chance that the seal will be swept under the ice before it can be retrieved. Such hunting was the standard technique before the introduction of the rifle, but now most of the hunting is done at open leads where the seals can be retrieved with a minimum of difficulty. In winter seals have a thick layer of fat and almost invariably float after being shot. Hunters will resort to waiting at breathing holes only when there is no open water within traveling distance of the village.

A seal's breathing hole appears as a raised knob on the surface of the ice and contains a small opening through which the seal's nose can be seen when it comes up for air. The hunter stands over the hole and attempts to shoot the seal in the head so as to kill it instantly. The shot breaks the ice enough so that it is sometimes possible to hook the seal immediately before the current can carry it away. Then, after the seal has been secured, the hole can be widened for the purpose of hauling out the animal. Breathing holes are found where the ice is very thin or new, usually at places where leads have recently frozen.

Several generations ago seal nets were introduced from Cape Prince of Wales and apparently were used extensively before the introduction of the rifle (Rainey, 1947, p. 255), but no one uses them today. Most men feel that this technique would be more risk and trouble than it is worth.

Winter seal-hunting equipment is not elaborate; it consists of a few essential items that can be easily carried by the hunter whether on foot or with a dog team. Opinions vary as to the most practical rifle for seal hunting, but .25-35, .30-30, or .222 calibers seem to be preferred. Many men own the Model 1917 Springfield .30-06 which was issued during the war to members of the Alaska Territorial Guard. This is a more powerful rifle than is needed for seal hunting and the ammunition is expensive. Next to the rifle, the most important piece of equipment is the drag line (niksik) and its associated hooks for retrieving dead seals. This consists of a considerable length of braided nylon line with approximately three feet of sealskin line fastened to the end, to which is attached a small bone or ivory shank with hooks made of sharpened nails projecting from four sides. A wooden float is fastened directly below the shank. At the other end of the sealskin strip is a small wooden toggle for grasping. When a seal has been killed and is floating

on the surface of the water the float and hooks are swung over the
hunter's head and thrown. Ideally, they should land just beyond
the seal. As the hook is drawn toward the dead animal, it is given
a sharp snap in order to imbed it so that the seal can be drawn in.
Closely associated with the dragline gear is the three-legged seal-
ing stool on which the hunter sits while waiting for the seal to appear. The entire gear can be folded in such a way as to fit in between the three legs of the stool and the whole makes a kit that is
worn around the neck along with the rifle. The seal hook with ice
pick on the distal end and a piece of rope for dragging the seal
completes the essential seal-hunting equipment.

The small boats described are not an essential part of the seal-
hunting equipment but are necessary when the leads are wide. Men
who do not have boats must borrow, and must give a share of their
catch to the owner. Some hunters do not have dogs; they must haul
their seals back to the village by hand. This is arduous work and
hunters with dog teams have a distinct advantage. Formerly no
dogs were used when hunting on the ice, because hunters feared
losing them when the ice broke up or moved out with a shift in the
wind or current. Today dogs are much more plentiful and teams
are used to take hunters far out on the ice and haul seals back to
the village.

The erratic movements of the ice around the Point Hope spit
make winter hunting dangerous. In late October and early November all the ice around the spit is new ice and not the old pack ice
from the north. Its condition is influenced greatly by the wind and
a hunter has to be continuously alert for shifts in wind direction and
intensity. A strong north wind blows all the ice away from the
south shore, a south wind blows ice away from the north shore.
The effect of the wind on ice movements is a factor that hunters
must consider at all times, but it is particularly critical in the
early winter when even a light wind may appear suddenly and maroon a man on the ice. In midwinter, after the pack ice has moved
in, a sudden change in wind direction or intensity can open up
leads far out on the ice and maroon hunters without their being
aware of it. If a hunter sees that the ice is breaking or that a crack
is widening, and knows that someone is hunting beyond that point,
he fires three shots to warn him to return to safe ice. If someone
is known to be marooned on moving ice the mission bell is rung and
a rescue party in a skin boat prepares to go to his assistance.
Several hunters active today have required such aid in the past and
they claim to have felt intense shame at having put themselves in a
position that required extra work and effort by many villagers.

During the winter months polar bears roam the ice around Point Hope. They follow the open leads looking for seals and are often encountered by the hunters. Sometimes it is necessary to give considerable chase over the rough ice before a bear is killed. When a hunter kills a polar bear he does only a rough skinning job, leaving much fat on the skin. The skin is then laid in the snow with the fur side down and walked on to stretch and soften it. In the nineteenth century, bears were hunted with bows and arrows and with stone- and iron-headed lances (Rainey, 1947, p. 256); but even today, when high-powered rifles are used, it is considered an exciting and dangerous activity.

When a polar-bear skin and meat are brought back to the village it is the sign for a general gathering of friends and relatives at the home of the successful hunter. Female relatives of the hunter and other women come to help with the scraping of the skin while their husbands sit around and talk over the details of the kill and the children play together. A big pot of boiled polar-bear meat is usually supplied and everyone helps himself from time to time. The scraping of a skin is an arduous job and requires several hours of steady work by two or three women; then the skin is stretched outside and allowed to dry thoroughly. During the winter of 1955-56 more than thirty-five bears were killed; the previous winter, nearly seventy. The skins are sold to the village store at the rate of $10.00 per foot and are thus the most important source of earned money during the winter months.

Beginning in early December, white foxes are plentiful on the sea ice. Like polar bears, they follow the open leads; they look for seals that the bears have killed. A bear, unless extremely hungry, will eat only the fat on a seal; white foxes eat the rest. Hunters set traps for these animals on the north side of the spit; a south wind is less common than a north wind and there is less chance of losing the traps. Size one and one-half traps seem to be the best for foxes, and these are set near dead seals and secured by poking a hole through the ice in two directions, looping the chain around the ice, and tying the chain. Fox skins formerly were worth from $40.00 to $60.00 each but in 1955-56 the hunter was fortunate to receive $20.00 at the village store for one. Foxes are not hunted nearly so extensively as they were fifteen or twenty years ago, at which time they were the most important source of income.

Tomcod, small arctic fish traveling in large schools, arrive at Point Hope in January and can be taken through holes in the ice off the north shore of the spit. Women and old people do most of the fishing; they are joined on the weekends by children of all ages.

On a good day one person can fill a 100-pound coal sack with these small fish. The equipment for tomcod fishing consists of from ten to twenty feet of heavy nylon or baleen line with a sinker of ivory, metal, or other heavy material at the end. Dangling from this sinker is a cluster of barbless hooks. The line is fastened to a short slender stick held in the right hand; a guide stick is held in the left. The fisherman jigs his line up and down with short jerks for a few minutes, then jerks up suddenly and reels the line in rapidly by winding it around the two sticks, the pole and line guide. Several of these small fish are usually impaled on the hooks. They freeze rapidly and are eaten while frozen.

In late February and early March, crab fishing becomes an important part of the daily routine for women and old people. The small crabs are found on the south side of the spit and in much deeper water than the tomcods. The technique for taking crabs involves the use of a flat circular wire grid fastened to a length of nylon line. A seal's nose or a piece of seal meat is securely fastened on the grid, which is then lowered into the water through a hole in the ice and allowed to rest on the bottom for ten to twenty minutes. When it is drawn up there are sometimes twelve to fifteen small crabs and a few starfish attacking the meat. The starfish are discarded, while the crabs freeze and are eaten raw. Crab fishing continues well into the spring whale-hunting period. Together with tomcods they provide variety to the monotonous diet of seal meat during the winter months. Tomcod- and crab-fishing techniques are essentially the same today as they were in aboriginal times.

During the winter months nearly every able-bodied man hunts seals from daylight to dark every day. All other types of winter hunting and fishing are subordinate to the main task of securing as many seals as possible for food, fuel, dog food, and clothing. The best hunters—those who are on the ice at every opportunity—sometimes kill as many as 125 seals in the most productive period, the three midwinter months. It is difficult to overestimate the importance of the seal to the Point Hope Eskimo. Its flesh provides the main source of food throughout the winter for both people and dogs. Its fat is a cheap, efficient fuel for heating homes, and the skins that are not kept for home use can be sold to the village store where they bring from $1.25 to $1.50 each.

Occasionally in late February or early March caribou come close enough so that some hunters feel it is worthwhile to make the required two- or three-day trip inland, up the Kukpuk River. Often several hunters with dog teams will leave the village sep-

Plate II-A. Spring Whaling Feast

A successful whaling crew

An umelik *distributes* muktuk

Plate II-B. Spring Whaling Feast

The skin toss

Drummers seated under an upturned umiak

Dancing

arately, with arrangements to meet at a place in the general area
where the caribou are thought to be located. Here they make camp,
from which they range in search of the animals. The people are
hungry for caribou meat at this time of the year and most men
with teams make the trip.

Early Spring

Interest in the coming whaling season is first manifested during
the spring whaling feasts which usually occur early in March. The
sponsorship is by certain whaling captains, as explained previously. At these feasts, which are held for all the villagers, the
participants partake of the whale's tail, which has been saved especially for the occasion. The feast is called *angeerook* and formerly was held in the ceremonial house. Informants provide no
explanation of the feast except to say that it has always been done,
probably to bring luck in the coming season's hunting.

People begin gathering at the home of the successful captain
early in the morning and seat themselves on the floor around the
whale's tail which rests on an old boat cover in the center of the
room. The captain acts as master of ceremonies and when all the
people are present—they bring their own dishes and knives—he
makes a speech about the tradition of giving the feast, explaining
that the whale's tail really belongs to all the people. A prayer is
then offered, followed by a recitation of the Lord's Prayer by the
entire gathering. The members of the whaling crew then begin to
cut up the tail. For the captain, a strip about four inches wide is
cut off the already detached end. (The tail flippers were eaten at
the whaling feast of the previous spring.) Then long strips are cut
off each side of the tail for the crew. The remaining skin is removed, with blubber attached, in small sections about six to eight
inches square and the meat is similarly cut. While the cutting is
going on the captain relates stories of past whaling seasons, much
to the enjoyment of everyone present.

After the tail is cut up, the crew members sit down and their
wives and other women cut the meat into smaller pieces to be distributed to the people. The captain who is host is served first,
followed by the other captains. Then everyone passes forward his
plate to receive his share of meat, blubber, and skin *(muktuk)*.
Not all the villagers can be present, but at least one member of
each family manages to attend and takes home portions for the rest
of the family. Most people leave as soon as they have received
their portions but some stay to eat and visit. Thus the ceremony

is more of a food distribution than a true feast. All day long people continue to come and receive parts of the whale's tail to take home. Later in the same day the host and his crew members clean and repair their whaling equipment.

The basic whaling equipment consists of the skin boat *(umiak)*, paddles, a pair of oars, two or three sealskin floats, heavy rope, darting guns, and bombs. The paddles, oars, and darting-gun shaft are scraped clean to make them look bright and new, a survival from aboriginal times when it was considered that clean whaling equipment would please the whale so that it would allow itself to be killed. The darting guns themselves are greased and cleaned and bombs are repaired or reloaded.

Plugs and toggles are lashed to the sealskin floats and these are inflated. This work is done at the house of the captain on the day of the whale-tail feast; tea, crackers, and other food are served to the working crew members by the captain's wife. Crew members are not paid for this work because it is considered to be one of their whaling duties. Other crews clean and repair their whaling equipment at about the same time that they put the skins on their boats.

Under aboriginal conditions the Eskimo used an ordinary harpoon rather than the darting gun. It was provided with a large ivory toggle head for striking; long flint-headed lances were used to complete the killing. The first commercial whalers introduced the shoulder gun, which fired a bomb into the whale but necessitated the use of some form of harpoon afterward for attaching the wounded animal to the boat. The darting gun was invented about 1880 by two New Bedford whaling men for the purpose of whaling in the Arctic where there is a chance that the whale will escape under the ice when hit with a common harpoon or fired at with a shoulder gun (Tower, 1907, p. 84). The darting gun consists of a tubular barrel, approximately twenty-six inches in length, which is fastened to a six- or seven-foot wooden shaft (Fig. 1). On one side of the barrel is a series of rings (A) for the attaching of a heavy iron harpoon. On the other side, a slim metal rod (B), which extends beyond the distal end of the barrel, acts as a trigger. A bomb is fitted in the end of the barrel. When a whale is approached it is struck with the metal harpoon. When this has sunk sufficiently into the whale's body, the trigger mechanism releases the bomb which goes deep into the whale and explodes. The harpoon then detaches itself, taking with it the rope and floats that are attached. The darting gun is effective if the bomb is well directed, its main drawback being that the boat must be very close to the whale before the weapon

can be used. A small firm in central Pennsylvania still manu-
factures the darting gun, bombs, and harpoons, mostly for sale
to the so-called primitive whale hunters of the world.

Figure 1. Darting gun

Some time during early spring, each whaling crew must put
the skins on their boat and make it ready for the season. This is
usually done in early March although some prefer the summer or
late fall, which gives the skins a better chance to dry and bleach.
The skins must be new and clean for whaling; if a captain puts his
skins on during the summer he may be tempted to use the boat before freeze-up, thus getting them dirty and worn.

The partially dried skins that the captain has been saving for
over a year are put through a hole in the ice to soak for a week or
two so they may become soft. When the day arrives for the sewing
there is a gathering of women and men at the house of the captain.
Usually eight women are there for the purpose of sewing. Some
are crew members' wives but most are the expert older women
who do the sewing for all the crews. The men, including crew
members and other interested persons, led by the one particularly
adept man who serves in this capacity for all the crews, decide
how the five skins are to be cut. The cutting pattern provides for
one skin lengthwise at the bow, another lengthwise at the stern,
and three crosswise between these two. In addition, at the bow
and stern are head skins sewn in such a way that the eye and ear
holes are visible at the two ends of the boat. When the cutting is
completed, the sewing begins and the men leave to work on the
boat frame. In sewing, the seams are made double, first on the
outside, the needles only partially piercing the skin. After the
first sewing, the women roll the skins and sew them as they roll
from each end. The whole process takes about five hours. The
captain's wife provides cake, bread, tea, coffee, cigarettes, and
candy for the sewers and others present.

At this time the boat frame is moved from the rack near the
captain's house to the National Guard building or the parish hall
where it is repaired; old nails are pulled and broken ribs are replaced prior to putting on the skins. Crew members do this work
with assistance given by others. All the sealskin lashing and other

materials needed for repairing the boat are provided by the captain. When the boat frame is completely repaired it is greased with whale blubber, presumably to make it possible to move the skins back and forth over it when fitting. In stretching the skins on the frame the bow and stern pieces are first lashed; then the side skins, starting at both bow and stern, are fastened with lines that pass over the braces inside the boat. As some men run the lines through, others draw up the slack to make the skin as tight as possible. The skins are very soft, pulpy, and pliable, stretching quite easily with lines that pass through slits in the edge. Occasionally, at the boat ends, a skin will not reach the gunwales and patches must be made.

The lashing is completed in about an hour. The boat is then taken from the building, placed on a boat sled, and returned to the rack near the captain's house. All the children of the village climb into the boat and ride until it is lifted onto the rack, at which time the captain's wife gives candy to them and they shout good luck greetings to the crew for the coming whaling season.

Historically the boat captain has held an important position in Point Hope village life. He was normally the wealthiest man in the large extended family that characterized village social structure, as well as being in charge of the whaling crew. His position and prestige were achieved through skill, energy, and the inheritance of property. Very often he was a shaman *(angatkok)* as well. His whaling crew was generally drawn from the men of his family; outside his family he had no real authority. However, during the autumn rituals in the ceremonial house, most of which were involved with the whale hunt, he and other captains were the leaders. As leaders in the ceremonies, the captains undoubtedly exercised considerable social control and disciplinary function (Rainey, 1947, p. 241).[2]

There were nine whaling crews at Point Hope during the 1956 whaling season, and of these, five captains acquired all or part of their equipment through inheritance. There are no rigid rules of inheritance; a man's whaling equipment or other property might be inherited by any one of his sons, his wife, or any other relative. Three present-day captains inherited the bulk of their equipment from their fathers, while one man acquired his through his wife's daughter's first husband, and another operates with equipment that actually belongs to his mother-in-law. She never has anything

---

[2]See also Spencer, 1959, pp. 177-92.

directly to do with the whaling activities but her ownership of the equipment is fully recognized.

In recent years it has been possible for some men to become captains on their own; this is the case with four of the present Point Hope crews. Money earned during summer employment has enabled more men to become captains. Occasionally whaling equipment can be purchased from someone who has left the village, or has decided, for some reason, to give up whaling. Recently one captain purchased equipment in this manner with money earned as maintenance employee at the school plus some borrowed from his mother. A Point Hope man who had moved to Fairbanks offered to sell a complete set of whaling equipment including darting gun, bombs, floats, flensing tools, and the like for $300.

A successful Point Hope man who obtained lucrative employment for several summers on various Alaskan construction projects decided to put out his own crew during the 1955 whaling season. He already owned a skin boat but purchased a darting gun for $175, five bombs at $15.00 each, four shells for the bombs at $1.30 each, two spears at $15.00 each, and $45.00 worth of heavy rope for the floats, a total of approximately $330 plus the value of his boat which he placed at $200. A person without a boat would thus have to spend over $500 for new equipment. Needless to say, few men can afford this expense and it is understandable that the term *umelik* is translated as "rich man" in modern contexts.

The Point Hope skin boats seat eight people, the optimum size for a whaling crew. Even so, some crews are smaller. A young man who led a crew for the first time during the 1956 whaling season was able to obtain only four full-time crew members and one boy who was out of school part of the time.

Formerly, although a captain drew most of the men for his crew from his own extended family, there was always keen competition among the captains to obtain the services of the best hunters. Today, the closely knit extended families are no longer dominant in the social structure and this is reflected in the composition of the modern crews. Only one captain relies heavily on members of his extended family. He is an old man and no longer active in whaling so his daughter's husband is acting captain. Other crew members are his wife's son by a previous marriage, his wife's brother, and two sons of his wife's brother. A granddaughter and his wife's brother's daughter act as part-time cooks. Another whaling crew is largely made up of members of a large nuclear family.

In most cases it is necessary for a captain to hire at least some of his crew members, with payment usually not in excess of $10.00, or a gift of comparable value. Family members are not paid but neither are they obligated to serve in the same crew year after year. There is always active competition for good hunters and it is not uncommon for a captain to make a payment or give a gift to one of his outstanding crew members at the end of the whaling season in order to be sure of his services the following year. Prior to the 1956 whaling season, some gifts to prospective crew members were a rifle, seals, ivory, rubber hip boots, and other items of clothing and food. Crew members, for the most part, seem to stay with the same crew year after year, but there is undoubtedly more moving around than there was in former times. Some men even mentioned that they thought it a good idea to change crews once in a while. *note alteration in obligations*

by

The captains have no special continuing obligations toward the *whaling* crew members as they did under aboriginal conditions. A captain may perform favors or services for a crew member at one time *captain* or another but these are considered as part of the payment. The wife of one crew member, who lacked bearded-seal skin for boot *(mukluk)* soles, obtained the needed material from her husband's whaling captain. When occasions arise, favors of this kind are often granted by captains.

The captains are obligated to provide food for crew members throughout the whaling season; this may prove to be a considerable expense. If the captain has had successful hunting during the winter, most of the food may come from the meat stored in his underground cache. However, it is always necessary to buy tea, sugar, coffee, flour, and other such items. Captains estimate that it costs between $75.00 and $150 to maintain a crew through the season. Some men use money saved from summer employment for this purpose while others depend heavily on income tax refunds that frequently arrive just in time to be utilized.

From time to time the village council restates the whaling rules, which have been in effect for many years. A mimeographed copy of the rules is handed to each captain before the beginning of the whaling season. The rules, re-established by the council from year to year, are as follows:

1. All bombs and other whaling equipment should be marked with the captain's initials or some other identifying mark.

2. Any wounded whale that escapes and is later killed by another crew can be claimed by the crew making the initial shot if its bomb can be identified.

3. No individual is permitted to cut the whale for his own use without the consent of the captain.

4. The captain whose crew first strikes a whale must replace all bombs used by other crews to kill the whale, or, if all parties are agreed, he can pay the equivalent value in whaleskin.

5. The owner of block and tackle used in the butchering operations must receive a full crew member's share of whaleskin for use of the equipment.

6. Hunters must not hunt or in other ways cause disturbances east of the whaling camp and thus frighten the approaching animals.

7. If a wounded whale escapes, the captain whose crew made the first strike need not replace the other bombs used.

8. One fourth of the baleen of a wounded whale that has lost its floats but is eventually killed by other crews, can be claimed by the crew that first succeeds in attaching new floats. (This rule was more important in the days when baleen had a high value.)

9. If all boats are on the ice, the order of sharing the whale is determined by arrival at the scene of the kill or participation in the kill. If some boats are not on the ice, a representative may be sent to the scene of the kill to claim its crew's share. (Several years ago various council members tried to get the council interested in a rule that would prohibit boats that were not on the ice at the time a whale was killed from sharing in the whale. There was no sentiment in favor of this change and the rule remains as stated above.)

These are the major whaling rules, but the council occasionally makes decisions concerning other aspects of whaling. It is a common practice for families from Noatak, Kivalina, and Kotzebue to come to Point Hope during the season to take part in the whaling activities and to visit friends and relatives. The men occasionally join whaling crews for varying lengths of time and the council has established the rule that these men can receive no more than half a crew member's share unless they work with the crew for the entire season.

Toward the end of March, the first snowbirds are seen near the village and the people then know that the whales will soon follow. There is a definite lull in hunting activities before whaling begins, as seals are not particularly plentiful and everyone is anxiously waiting for the arrival of the whales. There is a great deal of discussion as to whether anyone has seen belugas, the size of the open leads, their distance from shore, and the wind, important considerations for the beginning of whaling. Belugas always appear before the bowhead whales and their appearance is the signal for the crews to go out on the ice. Formerly all crews went out at the same time after a consultation among the captains and old men. Today each captain decides independently.

Soon after belugas are sighted, and when wind and ice conditions are favorable, all the men go out on the ice with axes, shovels, and the like to make a trail for the boats. Shortly after most of the boats are taken on the ice for the first time. The captain and his crew members remove the boat from the rack and load it with supplies for the whaling camp. These include a cookstove with pipe, cooking utensils, food, tent, lamp, and gasoline stove. The whaling equipment is also placed in the boat. While the boat is being loaded it rests on the large boat sled in readiness for being pulled by one or more dog teams. Formerly, when everything was ready for departure, the captain chose an old woman to sing songs near a little fire built at the bow of the boat to bring the crew good fortune (Rainey, 1947, p. 258). Today an old woman says prayers while the crew members kneel around the boat. Then the dogs begin to pull and the crew runs alongside guiding it on the trail and over the rough ice.

All whale hunting is done off the south side of the Point Hope spit. As soon as a spot is chosen for the camp, the boat is drawn to the edge of the ice with the bow projecting over the water and blocked upright so that it can be launched at a moment's notice. The floats, paddles, darting gun, and other equipment are placed in readiness so that there will be no delay when a whale is sighted. A tent is pitched and the crew members rest themselves on the boat sled, which is covered with caribou skins and protected with a canvas windbreak.

The Point Hope people first began to use tents and stoves during whaling when they observed the European whalers doing this without any ill effects, at the close of the last century. People were at first shocked to see such luxuries on the ice, but when they noticed that the commercial whalers were successful, they quickly adopted these conveniences. Darting guns were also looked on with suspicion when they were first introduced. Even after the village crews had obtained them they were kept in the bottom of the boat and not used, because people said a darting gun would not kill whales. However, steel knives and lances were used in the killing and butchering of whales long before the advent of darting guns or shoulder guns.

The nine whaling crews are scattered for two or three miles along the edge of the water on the south shore of the spit, sometimes as much as two miles from land. Each crew has a cook, usually the wife of the captain or some member of his family, who prepares meals and does other chores around the camp. Each crew also has an older boy who acts as a sort of helper around the camp and who has been taken out of school for this purpose. He is a full-fledged member of the crew and takes his place in the boat when a whale is sighted. *Note - taboos*

In aboriginal times, the crews were allowed no sleeping bags, no tents or other shelter, no hot cooked meat, and no change of clothing until a south wind closed the leads and the boats returned to the village. Each man had a small water vessel made from a seal flipper and each crew had a tub of meat which was replaced from the captain's house on shore (Rainey, 1947, p. 259). Today, tea, coffee, and hot foods are used by all crews and most men bring some kind of sleeping gear onto the ice for the first two weeks of the whaling season when the weather is the coldest.

Ideally, the members of a crew spend all their time watching for whales and take turns sleeping on the sled. Actually, however, most crew members make frequent trips to the village and often at least one member and sometimes more will be away from the camp. Those in camp are constantly on watch for whales and have their rifles and shotguns handy for other hunting when no whales are in the area. Frequent breaks are taken for tea and coffee with biscuits, and one large meal is served each day, usually in the late evening. The boy helper is the busiest person in camp and his chores include doing all errands requested by members of the crew, making trips to town to pick up mail and additional food or clothes, keeping a fire going in the tent, and sometimes preparing food if the cook is not in the camp. Occasionally a crew does not have the services of a full-time cook, particularly if the captain's wife has several small children and must spend much of her time at home.

A mild north wind gives ideal whale-hunting conditions because it keeps the leads open on the south side of the spit but is not strong enough to cause dangerous ice conditions. When the north wind is strong it is necessary to choose the camp site with care because the ice may break, and boats and equipment are sometimes lost in this way. Under these conditions, the tent is erected on solid ice and the dogs are left there, too. Dogs are not brought to the edge of the ice even when it is safe because it is believed that the noise they make will frighten the whales. In fact, many people complain that there is too much running back and forth to town by dog teams and that this frightens the whales. Some old people feel that dogs should not be brought onto the ice at all; this was the rule in aboriginal times. However, most men wish to make frequent trips to town and therefore must have their dogs at hand.

The whale hunters remain on the ice as long as there is an open lead or large open ponds where whales can breathe. When the winds shift to the south and close the leads they go ashore for a much needed rest. At this time the boats are drawn up close to the shore on solid ice and set high on ice blocks to protect them from the dogs. Captains who have killed a whale are privileged to fix their paddles, blade up, along the gunwales to show that they have been successful.

Pursuing whales is exciting but considerably less dangerous than it might at first appear. Bowhead whales, not particularly large as whales go, frighten easily and do not thrash around when wounded or disturbed, but simply sound quickly and noiselessly.

When a whale is sighted fairly far out all the crews launch their boats and start in pursuit. If an animal surfaces close to one crew, that crew alone pursues it; other crews join in the chase only after the first crew has missed its chance for a strike. The harpooner sits in the front of the boat. As a whale is approached, he stands up and drives the harpoon deep into the animal's body. A trigger mechanism releases the bomb that explodes inside the whale. The animal then sounds, taking with him the line attached to the harpoon and the floats. All the boats gather in the vicinity of the place where the strike was made and wait for the floats to appear, a sign that the whale will surface soon. When this occurs, the boats rush in and attempt to affix another harpoon and bomb. Eventually the whale appears on the surface dead. Often one bomb is enough for a kill but the animal may remain under the surface for a long time before rising to the surface, belly up. Frequently, wounded whales swim under the ice and are lost.

The shoulder whaling gun was introduced at about the same time as the darting gun but never proved very satisfactory because of the necessity of harpooning the whale separately before or after it was shot. The darting gun has the advantage of combining these actions effectively in one maneuver.

Before the appearance of the American commercial whaling vessels in the latter part of the nineteenth century, whaling was overlaid with supernatural concepts. It was believed that success depended largely upon the use of certain hunting songs at crucial times during the hunting activities (Rainey, 1947, p. 260). The aboriginal whale-hunting harpoon had a large toggle head which

was thrust into the whale's body; the line from it dragged the floats
into the water. The floats tired the whale and forced it to surface
more often.

Today, a boat making a strike keeps away from the scene while
the other boats take over for the final kill. There is much competition between the boats for the second strike, since all boats share
in the whale and the share for each depends upon the time of its
arrival at the scene or the order in which the wounded whale is
struck. The first boat to strike gets the choicest share of the meat,
whaleskin, and blubber, and so on down the line. If it should happen that only one or two boats are involved in the actual kill, the
order of the shares for the other crews is determined by the order
of arrival at the scene, the harpooners of the crews touching the
whale with their paddles as they arrive.

The crews tow the dead whale to the edge of the ice. At the nearest point on the shore ice the crews disembark to cut off the flukes
that are to be eaten at the spring feast. Lines are then fastened to
the whale. With members of the successful crew in the lead, the
whale is dragged along the edge of the ice to some point close to
land where the ice is firm and considered safe for butchering. As
the carcass is towed, all men join in the "joy shout," a peculiar
barking sound something like the cry of a walrus. A messenger
is sent to the village and the mission bell is rung announcing the
good news. School is immediately dismissed and all the villagers
go to the ice to witness and to take part in the butchering of the
whale. Meanwhile, the crews return to their camps, where they
resume watching for whales, with the exception of the two crews
that struck the whale first after the initial strike. The latter strike
camp and go to the place where the successful captain has set up
his camp; here they take part in the butchering. While the other
crews maintain their watch some of their members also, from
time to time, may take part in the butchering.

The butchering begins as soon as possible and is completed
quickly in order to lessen the danger of the movement of the ice
and the loss of the whale. The successful captain raises his flag
over his camp to show that his crew has killed a whale. Each crew
has a flag, usually an American one. Some are very old, having
been originally obtained from the old whaling ships of the last century.

The butchering of a whale is a festive occasion and everyone
shows his happiness. The successful captain acts as host to the
whole village and fresh whaleskin is immediately boiled and served
to all those present. People look forward with a great deal of an-

ticipation to eating their first fresh whaleskin of the season. From time to time throughout the butchering procedure whaleskin is served, along with coffee, tea, biscuits, and doughnuts.

Each crew possesses a number of long-handled knives, flensing tools, and hooks. Before any cutting is done, however, the various shares of the whale are carefully marked off with a knife. The lower jaw is removed first and then the whale is gradually hoisted onto the ice with a block and tackle. Unless the whale is exceptionally small the whole animal is never brought onto the ice. As the meat is cut, it is dragged away from the scene of operations, and each crew stacks its share apart from the others so that it can be divided among the members. There is a separate pile for the captain of the successful crew.

The rules governing the partitioning of the whales among the participating crews are meticulously followed. The accompanying diagram (Fig. 2) shows the way in which the whale is divided. The

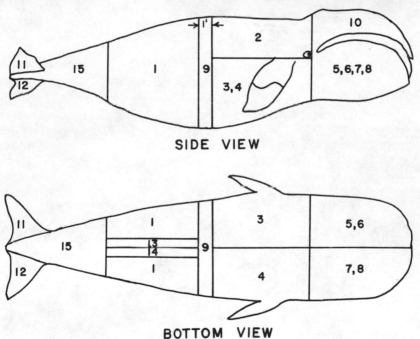

SIDE VIEW

BOTTOM VIEW

Figure 2. Diagram showing whale shares

section numbered (1) goes to the captain who first struck the whale, and is considered to be the choicest share. Number (2) is divided among the members of the successful crew. Numbers (3) and (4) are

Plate III-A. Whaling Activities

Butchering a whale

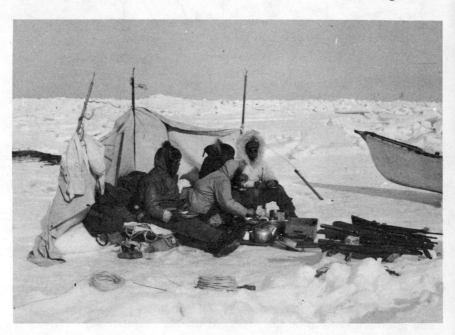

Watching for whales

Plate III-B. Whaling Activities

Butchering a beluga

An underground cache

divided among the members of the second and third crews to strike
the whale, and numbers (5) and (6) among the members of the fourth
and fifth crews. Numbers (7) and (8), the other side of the whale's
lower jaw, are divided among the sixth and seventh crews. A strip
as wide as a man's foot, encircling the body just behind the navel,
numbered (9), goes to members of the eighth crew on the scene. The
section numbered (10) is divided among all the boats and thus as-
sures the last boats of getting a share. Much of this section is eaten
on the spot by people participating in the butchering. The flukes,
numbers (11) and (12), are saved for the spring whaling feast, while
the tail, number (15), is eaten at the early spring or autumn feasts
already described. The *talayoke* section of the flippers belongs to
the captains of the second and third crews to strike the whale, and
is given by them to someone in their crews to whom they want to
give special recognition, usually the harpooner or an older person.
The *ingee* section, numbers (13) and (14), is cut from the navel to
the sex organs and is about thirty inches wide at the top and tapers
toward the tail. It is part of the captain's share and is often given
by him to his harpooner. Formerly, this section went to the captain's shaman.

When the butchering operations have been completed, each captain divides the meat, blubber, and whaleskin among the members of his crew according to his personal agreement with them.
Usually each crew member receives an equal share, the cook and
the boy helper also receiving a full share. The boat also gets a
share, and since it belongs to the captain he receives two shares.
If his wife is also the cook he does very well. After each crew has
divided its share, the meat, blubber, and whaleskin are hauled
away by dog team and stored in subterranean caches owned by each
household in the village. The whole butchering operation, from the
time the whale dies until the last meat is put into the caches, normally takes less than twelve hours.

The skull of the whale is returned to the sea, originally because
the skull contained the whale's soul, but today simply because "we
always do it that way." The baleen goes to the crew that first struck
the whale, and in aboriginal times it had many uses. Today it is
seldom used except by those who carve or weave baleen baskets.

When a man first becomes a captain with his own boat crew, and
kills his first whale, he is obligated by custom to relinquish the
captain's share and thus receives nothing. His share is divided between the second and third crews to strike the whale. Also, it is
the custom for old people in the village to ask for gifts from captains who get their first whale. They commonly ask for new boots,

and the captain usually takes the skins off his boat for this purpose. However, they may ask for anything, and when a captain killed his first whale during the 1956 whaling season, one old woman took his oil stove, another his rifle, and a third asked for and received a wolverine ruff. It can thus be seen that it requires not only considerable wealth to become a captain but continued wealth to retain the position after the initial success.[3]

Seals, walrus, and belugas are also hunted during the whaling season, although these animals are ignored if whales are running. Some crews fish for crabs, as well. Not many walrus are seen but occasionally one is shot from the edge of the ice. Belugas are difficult to shoot because of their continual movement and the fact that they do not expose much of their bodies above water at any time. To make matters worse, they almost invariably sink and the hunter must be fast with his dragline if he is to hook the animal before it goes down. If it does sink the hunter will often spend several hours in an effort to retrieve it with the dragline. For spring hunting of this kind, a weight replaces the float on the line. When a whaling crew is successful in killing a beluga, the crews located on either side of it send someone to help drag it in and butcher it. For this assistance these neighboring crews receive a share, the upper or head section of the animal. Beluga skin is highly desired but much of the rest of the animal is fed to the dogs.

Eider ducks and murres appear in great numbers in early May and are killed with shotguns as they fly over the whaling camps. Also, when a south wind is blowing and the boats go ashore, hunters take advantage of the lull in whale hunting to hunt ducks. They station themselves along the beach on the south side of the spit and wait for the flocks to come by. If a flock is flying low and close together, it is not unusual for a hunter to kill five, six, or even as many as nine with one shot. When eiders are plentiful a hunter may shoot as many as thirty in a day. Ducks that are not to be eaten immediately are put in the subterranean caches for use during the summer.

It is the custom that all animals and birds killed while a crew is on the ice are to be shared equally by all the crew members. However, this ideal pattern is not always followed. A captain was observed requesting permission of a crew member to use the blubber from his recently killed seal in the stove, and various crew mem-

---

[3] For a description of modern whaling by the Eskimos of Gambell, St. Lawrence Island, see Hughes, 1960, pp. 111-15.

bers were seen taking seals home to feed their dogs. This seems
to be the exception rather than the rule, and the custom of equally
sharing all game illustrates well the cooperative aspect of whaling. The crew operates as a unit when on the ice and only when
there is a surplus of game do individual crew members fail to
claim shares of the kill.

Early in June most of the bowhead whales have passed Point
Hope and the crews return to shore. Although the crews go out
early in April, they are not on the ice during the entire season.
The 1956 whaling season began during the second week of April
and ended about the first of June. The crews had been out less than
a week when a prolonged period of south wind kept them in for
nearly two weeks. At no time during the season were the crews
out for more than six days at a time. The season came to an end
because the ice was getting soft and rough water made operations
unsafe.

Factors that greatly influence the success of a whaling season
are the weather and associated ice conditions. A persistent south
wind can bring an end to whaling for long periods of time, while a
season in which a mild north wind prevails will give the hunters
every opportunity to stay out on the ice. Whaling conditions are
most favorable when the lead is not wide. The whales must then
pass close to the ice, making them easier to approach.

Bowhead whales were much more plentiful in the nineteenth century, before American whaling vessels began coming to the Arctic
about 1850. It was not uncommon, according to tradition, for as
many as fifteen whales to be killed in a single season. It seems
that the whale population should have recovered numerically in the
fifty years since commercial whaling ended, but today a highly
successful season means three or four whales taken. In 1956 two
whales were killed and three others were wounded. These escaped
because the bombs failed to go off, a fairly common occurrence
because the Eskimos load their own bombs and the powder is often
old and in poor condition.

Realizing that fewer whales are taken now than in the past, Point
Hopers are worried that the time may come when not a single whale
will be killed during a season. This has never happened in the
memory of living people. There is talk about too much running
back and forth to town and too many times when only a few crew
members are left in a camp. A degree of apathy was evident during the 1956 season on the part of some of the younger unmarried
men. They felt it was boring to wait for whales all the time. Many
hoped for a kill early in the season so that they might feel free to

take time off late in the season for other activities. On the other hand, some said that the crews were working harder that year than they had in the past, and spending more time on the ice in weather conditions that would usually be considered unsatisfactory for whaling. Only one whale was taken during the 1955 season and it was killed so late in the season that there was considerable worry about getting one at all. This may have been responsible for the sense of urgency that prevailed during the 1956 season.

Weekly movies, a popular event at Point Hope, for the first time were not shown during the whaling season so that the temptation to leave the whaling camps would be lessened. With a few exceptions, absenteeism during whaling is confined to the young unmarried men who often go into town, supposedly for just an hour or two, but, in fact, for overnight. This does not excite much visible anger on the part of the captains but several were heard to say that they did not want certain individuals in their crews the following year for that reason. Absenteeism often leaves the crews very shorthanded, so much so that they would be unable to give chase if a whale appeared.

There is considerable variation in the way the various whaling camps are operated. Some captains are strict and insist on things being done precisely as directed, while others allow their crew members much more latitude. In spite of the work involved, and the great investment in equipment, most captains are easygoing in relationship with their crew members. During the 1956 season only one captain was spoken of as being "bossy," but the main objection seemed to be not "bossiness" but the fact that he spent little time on the ice with his crew. People felt that he would have a hard time getting a crew the next year. Strict captains have well-organized whaling camps in which each crew member has specific duties at specific times. A varying degree of difference exists in the orderliness with which the various whaling camps are run but this reflects the fact that some captains are more particular than others about comfort on the ice and efficiency of operations.

At the end of the whaling season the successful captain chooses a day on which to begin the spring whaling feast, *nulukatuk*. Formerly, it began on the day that the crews came in from the ice; when the sun reached a certain point on that day all the crews came to shore. All the Point Hope people belong to one of two surviving ceremonial houses or groups, called *Qagmaktoq* and *Ungasiksikaq*. These organizations function even though the clubhouses with which they were traditionally associated have long since disappeared. In aboriginal times the captains of the former group drew up their

boats on the north beach, while those of the latter placed theirs
on the south beach (Rainey, 1947, p. 262). Today all the boats are
hauled up on the north beach and, as they have always done, the
captains from each group who have taken a whale during the season
just ended drag their boats across the point to the traditional places
where the spring whaling feast is held. The boats are elevated with
the bow facing the *nulukatuk* area, *Qagmaktoq* boats facing south
and *Ungasiksikaq* boats facing north. At the bow of each boat a pole
is set up with the crew's flag tied at the top. Formerly, the hunting
charms *(angoak)* would have been tied there (Rainey, 1947, p. 262).
The captain and those crew members who belong to his ceremonial
group arrange their paddles in the gunwales so that the blades point
upward. After the arrangement of the boat is completed, some
whale meat, biscuits, and tea are served by the successful captain
to the fellow members of his ceremonial group. Following this
there is a period of general conversation and relaxation, after
which some of the group members go to gather tarpaulins and other
equipment that will be needed for the following two days of the festivities.

The activities of the second whaling feast day begin in the morning when people gather at the location of the *Unagsiksikaq* boats
for the "fluke feast." The boats of the successful captains are
turned on end so as to form a windbreak and tarpaulins are arranged in a similar fashion. Old people have first choice as to
where to sit and some of them usually sit on the boat sled directly
in front of the upturned boats. Others sit wherever they choose,
although *Ungasiksikaq* members have the choice seats behind the
windbreaks; families generally sit together. After prayers by the
missionary, the successful captain stands before the gathering
near barrels of sour meat and the flukes from the whale that his
crew killed. The sour meat has been prepared in advance by allowing whale meat and blood to stand for a few days near the stove
in the Captain's house. His wife, with the helpers, hands out sour
meat to everyone while the captain himself, together with the members of his crew, cuts the flukes into sections. The captain, with
the help of his wife, then hands out sections to everyone present.
Each person is called by name and comes forward to get his share.
The calling of the names is accompanied by comments from the
captain and his wife about the person as he comes forward and this
causes much laughter and amusement in the crowd. The comments
frequently refer to personal characteristics or incidents and are
sometimes obscene. Apparently the fluke sections can be distributed in any order. During the 1956 feast one captain handed sec-

tions to the priest and his wife first, while another gave his first sections to an old man who had helped him when he was an orphan in Kivalina many years before. Old people, poor people, and orphans are always particularly well treated at the "fluke feast." People say that the captains have in mind that they must help the needy when they are celebrating their success in whaling. Great quantities of meat are eaten on the spot and the various families take home much to be consumed later.

On the afternoon of the same day, an identical procedure is observed at the traditional site of the *Qagmaktoq* ceremonial group. After the fluke sections have been distributed, preparations are made for the *nulukatuk* or skin toss. (The term actually means "skins for tossing," but is used for the ceremony as a whole.) Each ceremonial feasting place has four tripods of whale bone that are used to support the *nulukatuk* skin, a large walrus skin or series of bearded-seal skins with rope handgrips along the edges. Rope lines, fastened to stakes in the ground, pass over the tripods and are attached to a square framework of taut lines at the center, some three or four feet above the ground. The skin is then drawn tightly over the framework by lines, and twenty or thirty people grasp the handgrips along its edge in preparation for the tossing. Usually the first person tossed in the skin is the successful captain or his wife, particularly if the captain has killed his first whale during the season just ended. As he is tossed high in the air by the people holding the skin, he hurls gifts to the crowd. Formerly, highly prized objects such as furs, bundles of baleen, and the like, were thrown, but today the objects thrown are soap, chewing-tobacco, packages of cigarettes, and the like. Even so, there is a mad scramble to retrieve them. The jumping is accompanied by drumming and singing, and the jumpers are supposed to move to the rhythm of the music, a feat that they can accomplish if they do not fall when they land. The drummers are seated under the upturned boats. Following the captain and his wife, anyone who wishes may jump into the skin and be tossed. Women who have had a male child since the last whaling feast often throw small gifts from the skin, and formerly, women whose sons or grandsons killed their first animal of any species during the preceding year also threw gifts. Men seldom seem to toss gifts although they did in aboriginal times. However, the skin toss is mainly a sport calling for balance and coordination, which most people enjoy and at which they are amazingly adept considering that it is done only once a year.

On the third day activities begin early in the morning with preparations for a feast. People begin gathering at the traditional areas about nine o'clock, each person bringing food to be eaten at the feast. The men stay on one side of the area while the women prepare the food on the other and as the food becomes ready it is served to the men. The women eat on their own side and most of the younger children stay with them. The feast consists of whale and beluga meat brought from the subterranean caches, as well as a variety of store foods. It is conducted simultaneously by both ceremonial groups. The men occupy themselves with games and conversation while they are waiting for the various foods to be prepared. After several hours of feasting, activities at the *Qagmaktoq* area come to an end and everyone goes to the *Ungasiksikaq* area where preparations are made for the skin toss. Following the toss a dance is held, with the successful *Ungasiksikaq* captain dancing first, followed by members of his crew and then others. The dance brings the festivities to an end.

Formerly, the morning of the third day was reserved as a time to mourn for the dead. Early in the morning the captains visited the graves of people who had died the preceding winter, and left small pieces of whaleskin. At this time, too, relatives of the deceased mourned openly and helped to place the bodies, which had been temporarily buried in the snow, on scaffolds of driftwood poles and whale jawbones (Rainey, 1947, pp. 262-63). Otherwise, the spring whaling feast remains today much as it was prior to European contact.

The whaling feast is the last remaining ceremonial event at Point Hope that exists in context and has meaning as far as Eskimo culture is concerned. It signifies the end of the whaling season and emphasizes the participation of the entire village in this important activity. At the same time it emphasizes the prestige to be gained from killing a whale and reinforces the captains' positions as prominent men in the village. Even a captain who has just killed his first whale, and therefore suffers financial loss rather than gain, nevertheless achieves the prestige of being a successful whaling captain.

Many years ago, the old people say, bowhead whales passed by the Point Hope spit in the fall on their return migrations southward. At that time there were two whaling seasons each year as there are at Point Barrow today (Rainey, 1947, p. 263).

Late Spring

Following the spring whaling feast men turn their attention to hunting seals. Spring seal hunting begins about the first of June when the ice starts to break up and there are small leads and open ponds close to shore. Under these conditions, seal and bearded-seal hunting is good, and continues through June into July whenever a south wind keeps the ice close to the shore on the south beach. The small spring seals can be hunted from shore, the hunter sitting on the beach with a .22 caliber rifle. A rifle of larger caliber is kept handy in case a bearded seal or walrus is encountered. Hunters take their small skin boats to retrieve seals shot some distance from shore, and also to use as a blind behind which they sit when on shore. Seals and bearded seals do not have a heavy fat layer in late spring and consequently great numbers of them sink when shot. The dragline, with a weight rather than a float, is used to retrieve them. A great number of seals are killed at this time of the year, it being not uncommon for a man to get fifteen to twenty in one day. These are stored in the subterranean caches and are practically the only source of dog food during the late summer and early fall.

In 1956 there were strong north winds through much of June, keeping the ice offshore. By the end of the month, it was obvious that the ice was not going to return. Thus, for the most part, the village was deprived of the spring-seal and bearded-seal hunting on which it depends so heavily to carry through summer and early fall when there is little or no sea-mammal hunting. The skins of the bearded seals killed at this time of year are used for boot soles and also to cover the skin boats for the next spring's whale hunt.

Beginning around the first of June a few families move into canvas tents located along the south beach. More move as the spring season continues. After the whaling feast some people move as far as Jabbertown where the ice remains longer than at Point Hope and the spring seal hunting is particularly good. Often in cases where large extended families occupy a single house part of the family will move into a tent for the summer. The Point Hope people look forward to moving into tents and sometimes they are erected adjacent to houses. In the old days the semisubterranean houses became damp and foul smelling during the summer, and were often partly filled with water. The desire to spend the late spring and summer in a clean, light tent has persisted in spite of the change in house type.

Walrus hunting is not generally good at Point Hope, although these animals are said formerly to have hauled up on the beach during the summer where they were killed in great numbers. Normally, in recent years, a few are killed during the whaling season and perhaps one or two during the summer as they swim offshore.

It has been more than twenty-five years since the animals hauled
up on the beach in any great numbers.

In 1956 several herds of female walrus passed along the south
side of the spit about the middle of June and the hunters were quite
successful in killing them. Although the animals were close to
shore, it was necessary to go by boat to a fairly large piece of
floating ice, establish a station, and wait for the walrus to raise
their heads above water. Walrus sink immediately after being shot
and the hunter must be skilled in the use of the dragline if he is to
retrieve most of the animals he kills. A walrus is cut up without
being skinned and the pieces of meat and blubber are tied together
in such a way that the skin covers the whole outside area, thus af-
fording protection when the meat is placed in cold storage.

Sea birds continue to migrate past the village in large numbers
during June and July. Flying northward, they follow the south shore
of the spit to the end and then cut across at the very tip. Hunters
with shotguns station themselves at this point and kill great numbers of birds. Many of these are placed in the subterranean caches
to be eaten during the late summer and fall.

Two methods of seal hunting formerly practiced during the spring
have not been carried out to any great extent since the introduction of the rifle. Hunters no longer stalk seals as they lie on the
ice, nor do they place nets below the enlarged breathing holes
(Rainey, 1947, pp. 263-64). Like winter breathing-hole hunting,
these methods are not so rewarding as hunting at open leads.

Summer

Summer is a time of relative inactivity in the village compared
to other seasons of the year. Once the sea ice has gone, there is
little or no sea-mammal hunting of any kind. Many of the men leave
the village to seek employment in Fairbanks, Anchorage, and other
Alaskan cities, or at the various military sites that are in process
of construction along the Arctic coast. Some leave the village soon
after the spring whaling feast but most stay to take advantage of
the late spring seal hunting.

Opportunity for employment outside the village during the relatively inactive summer months is a recent addition to the yearly
cycle, although as early as 1906 a few men were leaving the village during the summer to work at the mines near Candle. Climatic conditions in Alaska, which confine most building construction and other outside work to the summer months, are ideal from
the Eskimo standpoint as they permit the men to earn a cash in-

come at a time of the year when there is little else to do. It does not interfere with their hunting activities, upon which they are still dependent for most of their food. The uneasy peace that has existed between the United States and Russia since the end of World War II has resulted in increased defense construction in the Arctic, and as a result the chances for Point Hope men to earn cash have been improving over the past few years and may be expected to continue to improve.

During the summers of 1951-53 there were opportunities for about thirty men to work on a radar station being constructed at Cape Lisburne, about fifty miles north of Point Hope. Many men joined a building trades union at that time, a factor that has contributed greatly to their subsequent success in obtaining summer employment. Most Point Hope men are well aware of the advantages of union membership and try hard to keep up their monthly dues payments even during the winter months when cash is scarce. A few men have become skilled carpenters and a scattering of other unions are also represented in the village. By communicating with the office of the union local in Fairbanks, it is possible for a man to be sent directly to the location of employment. It is not required that a man make the trip to Fairbanks to be hired "off the bench" there.

Point Hope men have been going to Fairbanks and Nome during the summer for a number of years to work for a mining company that carries out gold mining operations. This is still the chief employment opportunity for nonunion men, although the relatively low wage scale, combined with expensive transportation, cuts down considerably the amount of money that a man is able to bring back to the village. Some nonunion employment is also available in Kotzebue and Point Barrow. Often it is possible for a man to combine longshoring or other work in these villages with ivory carving for sale to tourists.

Some of the young Point Hope men have had a surprising amount of labor experience considering the relative isolation of the village and the lack of employment opportunities until recent years. A typical example is a young man who left the village in the summer of 1950 to work for the Alaska Railroad at Fairbanks. Rather than return to Point Hope, he went to Anchorage in the autumn, where he obtained employment at a local filling station and garage. In midwinter he returned to Fairbanks and worked for the Alaska Railroad, staying on the job until spring. During the summer of 1951, he obtained work on a government construction project near Fairbanks and joined the union, but was released in midsummer.

After living in the city until most of his money was gone, he obtained a job as dishwasher at a nearby air base and joined the restaurant employees' union, paying his dues with his first month's pay. Later in the summer he was transferred to Cape Lisburne and from there returned to Point Hope in the autumn. The following spring he went to Kotzebue and was employed on a seagoing tug headed for Seattle. He "jumped ship" in Seward and eventually worked his way back to Point Hope during the winter of 1952 (VanStone, 1958a).

The preceding account cannot be considered as typical of the employment history of all Point Hope men, most of whom prefer to return to the village every fall, but it does show the variety of employment possibilities open to villagers and taken advantage of by those young men with a good command of English and without close family obligations. Employment opportunities within the village are extremely limited and consist mostly of occasional part-time work at the school or mission. The only individuals with full-time employment in the village are the postmaster, storekeeper, assistant storekeeper, and maintenance employee at the school; the mission interpreter is paid for approximately twenty hours of work per week. Occasional full-time or part-time employment opportunities for women are available at the school.

For those who do not leave the village in summer there are a limited number of food-getting opportunities. Toward the end of June, caribou come down out of the mountains and range along the coast. Quite a number can be taken by men traveling along the coast in outboard-powered skin boats or by those making a trip to the mouth of the Kukpuk River. Usually a captain with a boat, joining with someone who has a motor if he lacks one, organizes a team with several other men for a three- or four-day trip. It is not unusual for a boat to bring back twelve or fourteen caribou. All animals killed are divided equally among those making the trip, except that the owners of the boat and the motor each receive an additional full share. Thus a man who owns both boat and motor receives three shares. An outboard motor is a particularly valuable investment under these circumstances, and can pay for itself in one or two years.

About the first of July boats leave for Cape Lisburne to the north and Cape Thompson to the south to gather murre eggs. These birds nest by the thousands on the cliffs, each laying a single large egg. The eggs are collected by climbers on the cliffs, the hunter wearing a loose-fitting parka-cover in which he gathers the eggs, descending to unload as necessary. Many boats combine egg gathering with caribou hunting. A camp is made on the coast for a few days of inland hunting. The eggs are divided equally among all members of the party with extra shares for the owner of the boat and motor.

Beginning late in July and continuing through August, a few people fish with nets along the north beach close to the village. The fish move close to the shore and the nets are set out with the aid of a long pole. The fishermen seat themselves along the shore. When a school is sighted everyone throws stones to drive the fish into the net, whereupon the net is drawn in and the fish are thrown out on the ground. Various kinds of salmon and a variety of sea trout are taken. Fishing is not particularly rewarding at Point Hope and not many people find it worth while to engage in this activity. Catches vary from one fish to thirty or forty, but it is seldom that more are taken at one time. *note prior tendency to*

Formerly, Point Hope families left the village during the summer months to a much greater extent than they do today. Some *hope* traveled down the shore to fish and net belugas while others made *during* extensive trips into the interior for caribou. As recently as fifty *fall* years ago, many families traveled to a center near the present village of Kotzebue where they traded with inland Eskimos from the Noatak, Kobuk, and Selawik rivers, as well as with coastal peoples from Wales, Diomede Islands, Port Clarence, and East Cape, Siberia. The coastal people traded seal oil, whale oil, seal and walrus hides, and ivory to the inland people for furs, dried fish, jade, and other inland materials. A lively trade in ammunition, rifles, glass beads, tea, lead, drilling, tobacco, and alcoholic beverages was also carried out (Rainey, 1947, pp. 267-68; U.S. Census Bureau, 1893, p. 137). Russian trade goods reached Alaska from trading posts on the Anadyr River as early as the middle of the seventeenth century, and trading posts established by the Hudson's Bay Company at the mouth of the Mackenzie River in the nineteenth century brought English trade goods to northern Alaska.

Such is the yearly cycle of subsistence activities on which the economy of the Point Hope people is based. Although some of the specific techniques are different, the cycle itself, with the exception of summer employment outside the village, has not changed greatly during more than 100 years of direct contact with European culture. Basically, the cycle is still much the same as it was in prehistoric times.

Unlike some villages along the Arctic coast, Point Hope has a sense of unity and cohesiveness. The people definitely feel themselves to be members of a functioning group. As pointed out earlier, there is considerable community spirit, based, at least in part, on the fact that Point Hope is one of the few villages on the coast with historical depth, having been the site of sizable settlements for at least 1,000 years and possibly longer. The seasonal cycle of food-getting activities also acts as a binding force because much of it, particularly whaling, requires the cooperative effort of everyone in the village. The people are quite proud of their position as one of the few whaling villages along the Arctic coast and also of the fact that hunting in general is better than in most other places. Everyone is agreed that Point Hope is "a good place to live."

The Point Hope people, along with most other Eskimos of the Arctic coast, are fully dependent on hunting for the bulk of their food supply. They also depend on hunting to feed the village's large dog population, and most men hesitate to leave for summer employment until they have secured sufficient dog food to last through the summer and early fall. The cycle of subsistence activities, therefore, is of the greatest significance for community well-being. Although a fairly large amount of money may be earned during the summer months away from the village, the quantity of store food that can be purchased locally is limited and soon exhausted. Even apart from "luxury" food items, however, a certain amount of money for purchases in the village is a necessity: sugar, tea, coffee, flour, milk, gasoline for lamps, and ammunition are essentials, not luxuries.

In evaluating the character of the seasonal cycle in Point Hope life, it can be said that most men would rather earn their living by hunting than by any other means; but that the possession of a cash reserve, obtained through summer employment, takes some of the uncertainty out of a subsistence economy and at the same time makes it possible for them and their families to enjoy the luxuries with which they have become familiar through contact with European and American culture.[4]

----

[4]For an interesting treatment of sentiments toward hunting in another Eskimo community, see Hughes, 1960, pp. 132-36. A more detailed discussion of the significance of wage employment to the subsistence economy at Point Hope will be found in VanStone, 1960.

5

HOUSING
AND
SUBSISTENCE

THE ABORIGINAL house of the coastal Eskimos of northwest Alaska was constructed mainly of whale bones together with some drift logs. It consisted of one or more rooms connected to a passage to the outside. The floor of this passage was lower than that of the rooms. Access to the latter was through a trap door. Occasionally there were small partitions or other rooms leading off the passage. The main body of the house was not much below the level of the ground but the walls and roof were entirely covered with sod, giving it a dome-shaped appearance. A small skylight in the roof admitted light; a sleeping bench was usually located along the back wall; large clay lamps burning seal or whale oil provided heat and light.

This type of house, used by the Point Hope Eskimos well into the present century, had the advantage of being easy to heat but was cramped, dark, and had a tendency to become damp and unlivable during the summer months. The building of wooden houses at the whaling stations as well as the construction of the school and mission buildings familiarized the people with American building methods and created a desire for the new type of habitation.

Today there are no old-style houses remaining at Point Hope, although a few that closely approximate them are still occupied at the west end of the village contiguous with the Old Tigara site. One is constructed of vertical planks with sod piled all around it. It has a single-pane window in the roof. The tunnel, the floor of which is level with the house floor, is of plank and whale rib construction and has a turn at the outside end to avoid the prevailing winds. The house itself is no more than twelve feet square, and is occupied by a family of six that recently moved to the village from Point Lay. The house is a source of embarrassment to the occu-

Plate IV-A. Point Hope House Types

Plate IV-B. Point Hope House Types

pants. They would much prefer a roomier, lighter house of a "modern" type, even though harder to heat.

The first families to build frame houses found them drafty and cold with only the heat from a seal-oil lamp. Consequently they covered them with sod blocks, the result being a close resemblance to the old-style houses but without the tunnel. There are fourteen houses of this type in the village. All are equipped with large storm sheds at the entry, which serve not only as storage places but as protection from the strong winds, and which make the houses much easier to heat. Some men construct a second storm shed of snow blocks in winter for added protection. The entrances of most houses face either east or west because the prevailing winds are from the north and south.

In recent years the village store has stocked building materials. Every year the *North Star* brings shiplap, two-by-fours, rolls of roofing materials, plywood, and other materials for house construction. These materials are extremely expensive but there is not enough driftwood in the area to be of use to house builders. With these materials some families have built quite satisfactory one-room frame houses, with enough insulation that it is necessary to pile sod blocks only around the base of the house. None of the houses has a basement because the water level is only a few feet below the surface on the Point Hope spit. Despite improved materials for house construction it seems safe to say that few, if any, of the frame houses in the village would be livable were it not for improved methods of heating and new sources of fuel.

Most Point Hope homes, though simply furnished, have the crowded and cluttered appearance characteristic of dwellings occupied by a large number of people of all ages. The houses are dominated by the heating unit, in most houses home-constructed from an old oil drum, which is used for both heating and cooking. All families have at least one gasoline-burning pressure stove for quick cooking, heating coffee, and so forth, and for use in summer. The furniture normally consists of homemade wooden beds or iron cots set against the wall, crudely made wooden tables, and occasionally boxes or lard cans for chairs. There is shelf space for dishes, pots, and pans, and containers for food. Some families have shelves and cupboards ordered from the mail-order houses and sometimes chairs and tables obtained from the same source. However, most house furnishings are the work of the homeowners themselves.

The new and better built houses are finished on the inside with wallboard or plywood while the owners of older, less well-constructed ones often nail cardboard over the inside walls for added insulation. The floors in many houses are covered with linoleum. The walls are decorated with calendars, religious mottoes, and photographs of friends and relatives who no longer live in the village. Every house has a cross hanging over the inside entrance. Household luxuries include radios, hand-operated sewing machines, and gasoline-powered washing machines. The first two items are owned by all but a very few families, while the washing machines are relatively rare.

In the typical house, the beds are always against the wall and an attempt is made to keep the center of the room clear. Many families have no tables or prefer to eat seated on the floor with the food laid out on a board covered with oilcloth. The people do not use chairs or even chair substitutes to any great extent, but prefer to sit on the beds or the floor. Groups that gather to visit or play cards will invariably arrange themselves on the floor, as will men and women with inside work to do. Babies are occasionally placed in small canvas cribs suspended from the ceiling. This is a space-saving device and has the advantage of keeping the infant off the cold floor.

Most Point Hope homes are neat by American middle-class standards. Linoleum floors are kept scrubbed and as much orderliness exists as can be expected under crowded living conditions. Only three or four houses in the village contain more than a single room, and the necessity of carrying out all the functions of day-to-day living in one room complicates housekeeping considerably. Only two houses have toilets that are separated from the main living room. Most families simply have a chamber pot located in one corner of the room.

A variety of fuel is available for heating and the type used depends somewhat upon the financial condition of the users. The village store stocks coal, which is brought in from the continental United States on the *North Star* and is extremely expensive ($5.00 for a 100-pound sack in 1956), and also stove oil which is somewhat less expensive but still far from cheap ($2.25 for five gallons in 1956). At times in the past, coal has been obtained from natural outcroppings in the Cape Lisburne area, but it is of a poor grade and expensive to transport. Most people prefer, if at all possible, to heat their homes with seal blubber and will do so to the exclusion of other fuel when the hunting is good. Blubber is an efficient fuel and the homemade oil-drum stoves are particularly adapted for burning it. The blubber from a large seal will heat the average house for about a day and a half, perhaps two days if the weather is not too cold, while a 100-pound sack of coal lasts for about three days and five gallons of oil for only two in moderately cold weather. Commercial coal ranges can be converted to oil for about $40.00 by the addition of a carburetor. However, they are not suitable for burning blubber.

If a family can afford it the choice is usually oil or coal, particularly during the early fall when seal hunting is not good. At other times they burn seal blubber, which can be made to last longer by placing a piece of dried sod in the stove. An oil-drum stove can be used to burn oil without the necessity and expense of adding a carburetor, simply by rigging a five-gallon can above it and having a piece of copper tubing running into the stove. The oil drips onto a piece of dried sod and the flow is controlled by a small valve. By this method, of course, the oil is not used so economically as with a carburetor. This apparatus can be dismantled easily when seal blubber becomes available or money becomes short.

No one in the village, with the exception of the maintenance employee at the school and the postmaster, both of whom have a steady income, attempts to heat his house at night, and even during the day there is no attempt to maintain steady heat. The fire is built up and then allowed to go down and remain low for some time. If it gets cold in a house in the evening, or if fuel is low and must be conserved, the family often goes to bed to keep warm. This is particularly true of small children, who are sent to bed by their parents when the house begins to cool during the evening.

Often, in the late spring and summer, gasoline-burning pressure stoves are used continuously for heating the house. Again, finances determine how often this can be done.

Although seal blubber continues to be used for heating, it is no longer used for light. Gasoline-burning pressure mantle lamps are considered highly satisfactory and are used in every home. Occasionally, someone burns seal oil in an old can when short of money or if the village store runs out of unleaded gasoline, as it sometimes does in the late summer just before the *North Star* arrives.

The problem of obtaining an adequate supply of fresh water for drinking and cooking purposes is a difficult one because there are no streams or fresh-water lagoons in the vicinity of the village. The water table is only a few feet below the surface of the ground, but sewage and other refuse are dumped in the vicinity of the houses, hence wells do not produce water that is safe to drink. Several years ago, when a small military detachment was stationed near the village, a well was dug about one-quarter mile southeast of town and the water was tested and found satisfactory for drinking. With money collected by means of a sales tax, the village council purchased a pump and some pipe so that the water could be brought close to town. However, this well is open for only about three months, from July until some time in November. During the winter months the people depend heavily on snow for water, but in the early fall, when the well is frozen and there is not sufficient snow, ice must be hauled from a lagoon near Jabbertown, about six miles southeast of the village. During the fall months, fresh-water ice that has floated from the mouth of the Kukpuk River is gathered on the beach off the point. Fresh-water ice is easily recognizable from salt-water ice by color and texture. When the outside layers are chipped away, this beach ice makes satisfactory drinking water. Melting snow is the easiest way to obtain water during winter, although it is not entirely safe for drinking unless it has been boiled, a precaution which few people take. Some families go a considerable distance from the village to get their snow, where it is presumably cleaner, but others take it from close to their houses.

The Point Hope Eskimos are heavily dependent upon dog teams for hunting and transportation and most hunters keep a team of from six to twenty dogs. Two types of sleds are used, the old-style flat-bedded sled with heavy solid runners, and the light, built-up basket sled. The former is particularly satisfactory for use on the rough sea ice or for hauling a heavy load, while the latter is more successful on long trips. The basket sled was introduced about thirty years ago from the interior. With a large team of dogs it was especially useful in maintaining a trapline in the interior east of Point Hope in the days when trapping was an important aspect of the village economy. Formerly, both types of sled had bone shoes, but today they are of iron. Modern sleds have brakes but old ones did not.

Dogs in the village are not housed, but are chained to whale bones driven into the ground or to a large heavy chain stretched between two weighted oil drums. This latter method has the advantage of permitting the dogs to be moved easily according to the direction of the wind. Houses are not provided because they fill with drifting snow. The dogs dig holes for themselves in the snow and curl up for protection from the wind. Some people build elaborate snow shelters for their dogs, but use them only when the weather is particularly bad. They believe that to use them at other times will keep the dogs from being properly acclimated for long trips in bad weather. Since the dogs are chained near the house they are simply moved whenever the wind changes, so that the house itself can act as a windbreak.

There are more than 400 dogs in the village and the problem of feeding them can be particularly pressing at certain times of the year. Normally, a hunter depends heavily on the seals stored in his subterranean cache to feed his dogs during the summer and early autumn. However, there is often a time in the autumn when the supply of seal meat is extremely low and fall seal hunting has not yet begun. This is a period of semistarvation for most village dogs and it can be intensified if seal hunting the previous spring was not particularly good. Dogs are fed once a day and cooked seal meat is preferred because it goes further. If dog food is scarce, a man will cook a large pot of seal intestines and blood with much water added. In winter ten or twelve dogs that have been working hard will eat a whole seal each day.

Twelve dogs can travel fifty miles on a one-day trip if the load is not too heavy. They are harnessed two abreast to the towlines, although in aboriginal times the dogs were staggered up the line. Harnesses are made either of cloth webbing purchased at the store or of sealskin. A rigid padded collar of caribou skin stuffed with hair is a part of the harness. The people value a good dog at from $20.00 to $25.00 and a trained leader at $100 or more. Some men name their dogs while others do not bother. A relatively small amount of irritability is exhibited during the handling of dogs, although harnessing and driving may be accompanied by considerable profanity. An attempt is made to raise pups at least once a year, and a few are kept from each litter. No particular care is given to a bitch about to give birth, although occasionally a small snow house will be constructed around the place where she is tied if the weather is particularly bad. Bitches are highly prized and a man who has lost most of his dogs from starvation or sickness takes particular care of a bitch so that he may develop a new team.

A hunter without dogs is at a tremendous disadvantage because he must walk out on the ice to hunt and drag his seals back to the village by hand. He cannot move from open lead to open lead with much speed and has very little chance of being as successful as a hunter with dogs. Even so, there are several families in the village who are without teams because they have nothing to feed them or have lost them through starvation or illness. Some men keep only a few dogs and rely on borrowing from relatives when they make a trip inland to hunt caribou. Only the best and most indefatigable hunter can support a large number of dogs, and therefore there is considerable prestige involved in the size of one's team. It seems that some men keep large teams almost for the prestige factor alone, and take ten or twelve dogs for a short trip onto the ice where five or six would do just as well.

Foods eaten in Point Hope homes depend largely on the time of the year and the success of the household head as a hunter. All families greatly desire and relish some American foods and buy them whenever they can. The village store, which receives its shipments in the early fall, has the largest supply of food products at a time of the year when hunting is not particularly good and when families have the most money; thus the consumption of American foods is encouraged. The most popular food products purchased are crackers, pilot bread, peanut butter, coffee, tea, sugar, flour, canned and dried fruits, bacon, evaporated milk, candy bars, and seasonings. The store runs out of most of these items before Christmas and is unable to replace anything that is too heavy or large to be shipped in by air. Many of the older people regret that they have acquired a taste for American food because they know that when the supply at the store is depleted they will have to pay high prices for special orders from Kotzebue and Fairbanks. Flour is considered the most indispensable item; when the supply at the store is exhausted, the people feel deprived of a real necessity. Such an occurrence took place during the spring of 1956, and a large quantity of flour was ordered from Fairbanks by air. By the time it arrived in the village, the cost to the consumer was $11.00 or $12.00 for fifty pounds. Even so, the people bought it eagerly.

Products of flour are among the staples of diet and become even more important in times of meat shortage. Flour is made into a type of twisted biscuit that is fried in deep fat, either lard or seal oil. Some people like bread occasionally, and flour is also used as a thickening in soups and stews and is regularly made into bannock. Although pilot bread and crackers are eaten in great quantities, they are not considered an adequate substitute for products made of flour at home. Twisted doughnuts or bannock are eaten at practically all meals and often a family will have little else but this, together with tea or coffee, if the hunting is not good. Usually, however, a meal consists of some kind of locally obtained meat. All the villagers are extremely fond of meat and many old people do not consider a meal to be adequate without it.

The favorite and almost exclusive type of cooking is boiling. Meats obtained by hunting are almost always eaten boiled even though people are aware that there are other ways of preparing them. Ducks, owls, and other birds are made into stews and soups thickened with flour or rice, and many kinds of local meats and fish are eaten raw. A typical meal during the winter months might consist of boiled seal meat with seal oil, biscuits or doughnuts, tea, sugar, and sometimes jam. Coffee and biscuits or pancakes are a typical breakfast. Small children do not drink coffee although they may begin to drink a weak combination of coffee and milk or water when they are seven or eight years old. Children drink tea but the youngest usually have it diluted considerably with water. Everyone likes seasonings and the store stocks a wide variety of them, the most popular being salt, pepper, mustard, catsup, and meat sauces. People put a great deal of salt and pepper on their foods and enjoy mustard on boiled meat.

Meal patterns in Point Hope homes vary considerably and are influenced by the fact that during the school term the attending children receive a hot breakfast every weekday morning at the schoolhouse. Most families have only one large meal a day and the time it is served depends upon when the hunters in the family return. Breakfast and lunch are light, the heavy meal being served soon after the hunters return in the late afternoon or early evening. Coffee and biscuits or bannock are eaten regularly before retiring at night. Families eat seated on the floor with the food and dishes on a small, legless table. American-style dishes, cooking and eating utensils are used and most families have enough so that each person can have his own cup, plate, and utensils. Knives and spoons are used but not forks. Meat is picked up in the hands and pieces are cut off with a "woman's knife" *(ulu)* or a pocketknife of commercial manufacture. The women cut the meat for the smallest children, but girls especially learn to use the woman's knife at an early age. Sometimes a large piece of meat is put in the mouth and small pieces cut off one by one. After the meal is finished each person washes his hands and wipes off his knife. Tea and biscuits or doughnuts are then served. The women and older girls wash and wipe the dishes in warm, soapy water, but there is no rinsing.

Many Point Hopers are of the opinion that one of the things that has changed most in the village in the five-year period 1950-55 is clothing. Young people, particularly girls, are wearing American clothing much more than formerly. In 1950, the winter apparel of almost everyone included fur parkas and skin boots, very little American clothing being in evidence. Men still require heavy, warm parkas because they spend long periods of time on the ice in the coldest weather of winter. Furs of various kinds, most obtained locally but some ordered from fur supply houses in Seattle, are used. Caribou parkas are particularly warm and have the advantage of being made from a material that is readily available locally. Heavy cotton, wool, and occasionally fur pants and long underwear are worn in especially cold weather or during long exposure in such activities as whaling. Some men wear sealskin pants while others use the air force flight pants that are obtained from various mail-order army-surplus outlets.

Men prefer footgear of Eskimo types, such as sealskin and caribou boots in winter and waterproof sealskin boots in summer. However, American-type footwear has gained considerable popularity in recent years, particularly among younger men. Shoepacks are widely used and, in winter, Korea and "bunny" boots. Rubber hip boots have gained wide usage, as has rubber rainwear in general. The latter is admittedly superior to the old style gut garments but, in footwear, even those who habitually use the American types admit, when pressed, that Eskimo boots are better. The national guard uniform has been influential in framing opinions about clothes with the result that parts of the uniform are worn regularly by some individuals. Army-surplus clothing is plentiful in the village as a number of mail-order surplus houses make a special effort to get the small village trade. Although fur mittens are occasionally worn, men prefer pairs of canvas or cloth gloves as they give adequate warmth and allow freedom of finger movement for shooting. In particularly cold weather, gloves of this type are worn inside fur mittens. Women and girls favor knit gloves which often are made by hand.

The mission receives shipments of old clothes from time to time and these are sold to the villagers for low prices at rummage sales. Old fur coats are particularly desired because they can be made into fancy parkas. These clothes shipments contain all types of garments. Since they are sold very cheaply they allow many people to obtain items of American clothing that they would not otherwise be able to afford.

Many young men from sixteen to twenty-five are seldom seen in Eskimo clothing except when hunting. Even then they are more apt to wear national guard parkas and boots that are far from adequate. Even in the coldest weather they wear light pants, jackets, and low shoes, and often are obviously uncomfortable. Girls prefer American clothes when possible and dress in sweaters and skirts or dresses for church, movies, and other public events. Their ideas concerning dress styles, as well as the clothes themselves, come from the large mail-order catalogs. Home permanent waves are very popular, as are lipstick and all kinds of costume jewelry. Older women like dresses and skirts too, but wear their long parkas rather than jackets or light coats that give little warmth.

Everybody in the village "dresses up" for important ceremonial occasions. Women work hard just before Thanksgiving, Christmas, and the whaling feast, sewing new skin boots, parka covers, fancy parkas, and other dress clothes. Traditionally, everyone should have new skin boots for Christmas and for the spring whaling feast. Many people order new American-style clothes at this time and show them off at the public functions. A few of the younger men are greatly interested in dress clothes and have sizable wardrobes. Their tastes run to bright shirts, jackets, and ties. Girls, too, like bright kerchiefs and gaily colored blouses and socks.

Although men dominate the cycle of subsistence activities, women have a definite part to play. Men do all the hunting but women take an active part in hunting activities at all times of the year, and do most of the fishing. During whaling, women not only participate in the preparations when they sew the new covers for the skin boats but they are an integral part of activities on the ice. A whaling camp that has no woman to take charge of the preparation and serving of meals is under a considerable hardship from the standpoint of both efficiency and comfort. In summer when boats leave for Cape Lisburne to hunt caribou and gather murre eggs, one or two women are usually in the crew and take an active part in every aspect of the trip, even to the extent of doing some hunting themselves. A man and his wife frequently hunt caribou together during the summer months. Women do all the preparation of meat and skins and thus have a keen interest in winter and spring hunting. A man and his wife thus form an active partnership for carrying out the subsistence activities. A woman helps her husband in innumerable ways each day; e. g. , she may help him harness his dogs before he sets out to hunt in the early morning and be ready to aid him in unloading his catch in the evening. Many women have a keen interest in hunting, and in the past a few outstanding women hunters have been known (Rainey, 1947, p. 253).

Some families exhibit a marked degree of division of labor within the family itself. If a family is large and entirely dependent upon the success of a single hunter, everything possible is done to free him from activities other than hunting. Women and children often feed the dogs, harness and unharness them, and load and unload the sled so that the hunter can devote his full time to hunting and keeping his equipment in good repair.

When not hunting, men devote much of their time to the care and

repair of their equipment and the house. Women and children perform all the household chores and make trips for water or to the
subterranean caches for meat. In addition, women have food preparation and child care to occupy their days, but these activities do
not normally consume the entire day, even when the family is
large. If there are older children to help, a woman can usually
find time to visit friends or shop at the store.

Children always have many chores to do. Although the amount
of work demanded from youngsters varies considerably, it is not
unusual for boys or girls to be expected to get up first in the morning, build a fire, fill the pressure stove, and make coffee before
others rise. Young boys also help harness and feed dogs, get snow
for water, empty slop buckets, and perform many other chores.
Girls of ten or twelve ordinarily have less to do than boys although
they do help their mothers with housework to a limited extent. In
homes where there are a great many children, younger ones may
not have to help with chores for a long time, simply because their
parents prefer to have them out of the house so that older brothers
and sisters can get the work done more efficiently and quickly.

6

THE LIFE CYCLE OF THE INDIVIDUAL

IN THIS discussion of the life cycle emphasis will be put on the developmental and behavioral patterns of a normal individual. Deviations are mentioned when known facts serve to point up the discussion, but information is meager on marginal behavior generally.

As in most Eskimo communities, children are greatly desired at Point Hope and the normal adult woman is always a mother. There is a reasonably clear idea of the physiological causes of pregnancy, but contraceptives are practically unknown, are not understood by most people, and are never used. Forced abortion or curettement seems also to be unknown except as rumor, but some interest in the subject has been expressed by women involved in adulterous situations. It is generally agreed that male children are preferred but both parents welcome the arrival of a child of either sex. Most parents want many children, but some women would prefer but three or four. Apparently there are only two or three women in Point Hope who have not borne children. No reliable explanations for such barrenness were obtained.

Women take no particular precautions during pregnancy and there is no apparent concern over an approaching birth. Dietary restrictions are absent and the mother continues her usual chores until labor begins. However, if possible she avoids heavy lifting and carrying during the last weeks of pregnancy. Numerous beliefs exist concerning unborn children and a mother associates certain natural phenomena such as windstorms with the movements of the fetus. Also, the health of the mother during pregnancy is known to affect the child.

Young mothers have implicit faith in the ability of certain old women to describe the unborn infant and predict its future life. One woman related that when she was about six or seven months pregnant, she had a bad fall and feared that the child might have been injured. She went to one of the old women who felt her abdomen and claimed that she could still feel the child breathing. However, she further predicted that the child would be born very weak and would die before it reached its second birthday. The baby was born prematurely and did die before it was two years old.

All births are attended by midwives who form a professional group, although without organization. There are six midwives in the village at the present time and all are elderly women past childbearing age. All, at one time or another, have been trained in their calling by visiting nurses. This training is reflected to some extent in the procedures followed, particularly in the occasional use of antiseptics and a general attempt to maintain cleanliness. Several of the midwives attend each birth, one or two doing most of the work. Others watch, and give advice and help if necessary. Close female relatives of the expectant mother also attend.

All the women have learned to relate the frequency and regularity of birth pains to time of birth; thus they are able to call the midwives at the proper time. The men in the household arrange to be away from home. Apparently many mothers fear that there will be a great amount of pain with the delivery of their first child. Women who have had many children give birth very easily; occasionally the child is born before the midwives arrive. Women are sometimes in labor less than three hours. Breech presentations and other abnormal deliveries are known but do not seem to cause any great difficulties. One older woman, far advanced in pregnancy, was traveling by skin boat from Jabbertown to Point Hope. She asked to be put ashore "to go to the toilet" and gave birth after the boat had moved on without her. She cut the cord and scraped sand over the afterbirth, put the baby in her parka and ran up the beach to catch up with the boat. Another older woman who was pregnant went outside the house, ostensibly for a similar reason, and gave birth. She had to fight off dogs who smelled the fresh blood, but eventually got into the house with the baby. She was upset because the dogs had eaten the afterbirth.

Formerly, delivery took place in a kneeling position, but in recent years, midwives have encouraged women to lie on their backs. An elderly woman is said to have had her first three children in the old position and then switched to the new at the suggestion of the newly trained midwives. She has had three more children this way and seemed to have no particular preference for either position. Births are taken very much for granted and there is a minimum of disturbance in the family pattern of living by the arrival of a new child. If the delivery is normal and the mother in good health, she usually rises and resumes her regular duties within two days after delivery, sometimes sooner.

The household always receives a new baby with a great deal of joy and adoration. Children adapt readily to a new baby and take pride in being able to hold it. Even five- and six-year-old children are allowed to handle babies as often as they wish although a sharp eye is kept on them to see that no harm comes to the baby. Mothers like to play with their young babies but this demonstrative affection tapers off as the child outgrows babyhood. However, it was observed that three- or four-year-olds still receive considerable attention, particularly if they continue to be the youngest member of the family. By the age of four or five, though, a child is definitely receiving the routine responses reserved by adults for older children.

Houses with new babies are often kept very warm and yet there is no special attempt to keep the child warm. In the early months he may crawl around on the floor with practically no clothing even though the floor is the coldest part of the house. Often a diaper and shirt is all that is worn and sometimes the former is dispensed with. Conventional diapers, ordered from mail-order catalogues, are used and are worn past the age of two years or until toilet training is completed.

Infants and small children up to two years of age are carried on the back inside the mother's parka when outdoors. However, if the mother is in no hurry and the child is being encouraged to walk, he will be dressed warmly and left outside the parka. The birth of a younger brother or sister may shorten the time that a child spends in his mother's parka. When thus carried, a child wears normal underclothing. Sometimes older sisters or other young relatives carry children to help a busy mother. Small babies are also often placed in their mother's parka when they cry or fuss. A woman will stand in one place and sway back and forth as she pets the child, or she may walk around rocking and petting the child and sometimes singing gently to it. This usually has a quieting effect.

In the house, the small infant lies in a homemade crib, made from a wooden box, or a hammock suspended from the ceiling; or a bed may be used if no other place is available. If the child frets, he will be taken out of the crib. The mother stays near the baby at all times.

Infants seem to be kept quite clean. Most mothers change dirty diapers immediately. When a small infant starts crying, one of the first things a mother checks is the diaper. Older boys and girls sometimes contract impetigo but this seldom occurs with infants up to two years of age.

Small babies receive the breast as soon and as often as they desire and children up to two years are similarly favored if they have not already been weaned. In all cases sucking sessions are quite brief, usually not more than five or six minutes. Breast feeding is relatively undemonstrative; not much emotion seems to be involved.

The age of weaning varies considerably, depending primarily on the time of the mother's next pregnancy. Weaning takes place without any difficulty, because the baby is weaned to a bottle rather than to food. Infants continue to take bottles long after they are capable of feeding themselves. The bottle is a favorite device for quieting a tired or angry child.

Mothers say that their children begin to walk between the ages of one and two. Some infants were observed with well-developed crawls which probably retarded the age of walking. First steps elicit the same gratified response that is characteristic in our own society and children who are slow in learning to walk are encouraged by their parents to try time and time again.

A baby is allowed to play with practically anything that attracts him but he is protected from dangerous objects. As soon as the child is old enough to understand (about two years), he is told to release an objectionable article and some attempt is made to appease him by offering a toy, bottle, or some other desirable thing.

Children as young as six months were observed being held over a pot to urinate or held outside the house for the same purpose. There appears to be no stress placed on rapid toilet training although success in this regard on the part of the child is rewarded with kind words by the parents. A two-year-old boy was heard to say "toilet" and then went toward the can normally used for the purpose but urinated on the floor. The parents were amused by this "near miss" and the child, obviously partially trained, was given credit for taking a step in the right direction. Accidents seldom bring censure, although a three- or four-year-old child who should know better may be laughingly scolded for a minute or two while the mother is cleaning up. Parents do not seem to be particularly observant of cues that signify the child's toilet needs. A child of three is expected to be completely trained and an older child (six or seven years) who soils his pants or his bed often is severely scolded. A boy of nine who had an accident during school because the teacher refused to let him go to the toilet was severely

scolded at home, but the parents were also angry at the teacher.
A new baby is usually baptized within a month of birth and before this time it receives a name. Every child receives an English
name and at least one Eskimo name. These names, which are given
by the parents, are often those of recently deceased individuals or
deceased relatives. When English names were introduced thirty or
forty years ago, many individuals used their Eskimo names as
family names, or occasionally as first names. Some families took
the names of places where they had formerly lived as family names.
In recent years some people have felt the need to have shorter,
more pronounceable names, particularly those individuals having
dealings with the whites. Shorter names have been achieved in
some cases by taking the first name of an older relative, usually
the father, and adding the suffix *son* to it (thus, Frankson).

Formerly, it was believed that a child would cry until the right
name was found for it. Traditionally, a person who desired to have
his name perpetuated in a younger person would make his wishes
known to the family at the time of birth and the child would become his namesake *(komnaluk)*. The older person would make gifts
to his namesake from time to time, and would give instructions in
various activities such as hunting and esoteric matters concerned
with the supernatural. The older person considered that his spirit
survived in his namesake after death. Undoubtedly, many people
believe this today, although the namesake tradition is considerably
less strong than it once was. Namesakes are considered related
through the name and it is not unusual for a person to belong to the
ceremonial house of his namesake rather than that of his father
if the people involved so desire.

It appears that Eskimo names are used as terms of reference
and address much more frequently than English names. A Diomede
Island Eskimo, living at Point Hope during my stay, knew many
people only by their Eskimo names. Adults often use contractions
of Eskimo names when addressing small children.

Adoption takes place often since some families have more children than they can care for while others want more. In 1956 there
were fifteen adopted children in the village. Often a mother will
give her child for adoption because she is ill with tuberculosis and
unable to provide proper care. Even though parents apparently do
not make public announcements, it becomes known very quickly
that a couple is willing to give up a child. Sometimes it is obvious
that a family is in financial difficulty, in which case someone may
come forward after the birth and offer to adopt the baby.

In order for an adoption to be official, papers must be filled out and a fee of $25.00 paid. However, only two families have gone through this formality. Some who do obtain legal adoption papers for a child are primarily concerned with protecting themselves against the possibility that the parents may change their minds and request the return of the child. Occasionally parents do wish to have a child returned; this causes hard feelings. In recent years there has been increasing pressure from nurses and schoolteachers for legal adoption. Illegitimate children who are taken by grand-parents or other relatives must be officially adopted if the family wishes to be eligible for Aid to Dependent Children payments.

Grandchild-adoption is a prevalent form because parents miss their children after they are grown, married, or in school, and wish to continue to have children around them. Adoptions of this kind are nearly always unofficial. The child may be an infant but often the adoption takes place when the boy or girl is of such an age as to be of assistance to the grandparents. Frequently the adopted grandchild will be the only one in the family who can help the old people.

The adopted child enjoys the same position in the new family as do the other children and is treated just as they are. Children who are adopted by their grandparents often have to work harder than other children but there is no indication that they are not loved and well cared for. Some women feel that adopted children are more difficult to raise than one's own children, but this statement is usually made by middle-aged women who doubtless find child rearing more of a trial than it was when they were younger. A half-grown orphan who is adopted into a related family by necessity rather than choice occasionally becomes somewhat of a drudge and there are cases in the school files of complaints being brought against such families for mistreating or overworking the child. These situations, however, appear to be extremely rare.

Children form a large segment of the Point Hope population; there were 112 individuals under fifteen years of age in 1956. Small children stay close to their homes at all times. Between the ages of two and four they stay inside most of the time during the winter, but are allowed to wander close to their home in the spring and summer when the weather is good. They seldom venture more than two or three houses away and usually play with children their own age in the immediate neighborhood. The parents always know where they are and will occasionally look for them to make sure that they are all right. Often an older sibling will be responsible for a toddler to make sure the child does not wander too far.

When children reach the age of six or seven, mothers no longer

concern themselves with their whereabouts during the day. Older
boys and girls wander around in groups or alone and come home
only to eat. If there are chores to do, the child is told of them when
he returns; parents never search for a child to so inform him. Bedtime varies according to the time of year. There is a 9:00 P. M.
curfew during the period of school and children are supposed to be
at home by that time. However, few go to bed as early as that.
Some parents are more strict about bedtime than others, but in
most homes the children do not have to go to bed until they so desire. However, parents may suggest bed several times and remind
the children that they will have a difficult time waking in the morning if they do not go to bed. A threat will seldom be any stronger
than not to waken them in time for school. In the summertime,
children stay outside and play as long as they wish, often not returning home until two or three in the morning and then sleeping
late. Children do not feel it necessary to tell their parents where
they are, are going, or have been, and older girls roam around as
much as their brothers. It seems that opportunities for sexual relations are great although finding a secluded place is certainly not
easy.

Children eat readily and food is accessible to them as long as
it is available. Prepared food left over from a meal remains on the
table and a child may help himself whenever he comes in from
play. The adult members of a family often eat while the children
are out playing and no attempt is made to call them in. When they
come, they simply help themselves to what is left.

Adults always attempt to stop children from fighting and there
is a desire on the part of all parents to inculcate on their children
the value of nonaggression. "Don't fight" is a common phrase and
is often spoken most emphatically by adults. There is really no
acceptable outlet for aggression. Even wrestling is frowned on unless it is being carried out purely in the spirit of fun. Adults unrelated to a child seldom discipline him for fighting unless it is very
severe, or disrupting to some adult activity. Parents and older
siblings are expected to take care of it. Sibling aggressiveness
within the household is not tolerated and attempts are made to distract the small child who shows aggression toward others, older
or younger.

Children become aware of the facts of life and death at a very
early age, a situation understandable under circumstances where
a great many people of all ages live together in a single room.
Most children have seen a corpse by the time they are seven or
eight years old, and have witnessed their parents or married sib-

lings performing sexual intercourse. Two boys, approximately
eight years old, when visiting my house, lay on the bed and jokingly
imitated the position of intercourse. However, children do not
often joke or even talk about sexual matters, presumably because
it is so much a part of every-day observation as not to be worth
talking about.

It would seem that boys do not often play with girls except when
quite young. However, occasionally a large group of school-age
boys and girls will get together to play games. Boys prefer war
games based on events they have seen in films. They also like
games that demonstrate their physical prowess. These do not take
the form of aggression against another person, but are rather
demonstrations of their ability to balance themselves on one hand,
do push-ups, rise quickly from a squatting position, and the like.
Tests of strength with other individuals, such as finger pulling and
arm wrestling, are also popular. In the late spring and early summer, boys between the ages of six and fourteen or fifteen spend
much of their time shooting with slingshots at the small shore
birds that frequent the slough that runs through the center of the
village.

Girls do not play outside as much as boys, but when they do they
seem to enjoy most of the same games and activities. Children of
both sexes like magazines and, particularly, comic books. One
small boy informed me that he had injured his knee while imitating
Superman; he put a towel around his shoulders and plunged off the
roof of a sod house. Small children who cannot read enjoy magazines and comics as much as the older ones who, although they
have some reading proficiency, rely heavily on pictures and drawings for their pleasure. Play groupings of all kinds are generally
determined according to age, although there is considerable variation, particularly with the younger children.

Within limits, the behavior of male children toward one another
is largely determined by age. Older boys are privileged to tell
younger ones what to do, take seats from them at public functions,
force them out of games where the number who can play is limited,
and send them on errands. Younger boys always accede in these
situations, but not always with good grace. Young men have the
same advantage over older boys, but adult behavior is not struc-
tured in this manner.

The discipline of children appears to be relatively mild, although it is difficult to be certain since parents often seemed un-
willing to administer punishment in the presence of an outsider.
I was frequently under the impression that children were allowed

to behave in a manner that would not have been permitted if I had
not been present. Parents usually attempt to distract a child who
is misbehaving, and if a crying tantrum results they simply ignore
the offending child. I heard numerous parents threaten to spank
recalcitrant children but saw the threat actually carried out only
a few times. Small boys and girls are the ones who are most apt
to be spoiled and pampered, but once they reach the age of eight
or nine they generally obey their parents even if unwillingly. Children occasionally object strenuously to a parental decision and sulk
or cry for a long time, but do not wheedle or in other ways attempt
to get the parent to change his mind. Active, responsible participation in the affairs of the household is conducive to the early acquisi-
tion of an adult outlook and discipline plays a minor role.

It is difficult to detect the ways in which children learn the techniques of arctic living. Education is an informal process in which
the child more or less adopts the example set by older people.
There is certainly abundant opportunity for the observation of such
examples.

When a girl is nine or ten, her mother depends upon her for certain simple chores around the house and for help with the care of
younger siblings. A boy begins to be useful when he is about eleven
or twelve, although sometimes as young as eight or nine if he has
no older brothers. He will get up first in the morning to make
coffee, and will do other chores around the house such as filling
lamps, hauling water, and feeding dogs. A boy of twelve or thirteen can be of great assistance, leaving the adult males free to
devote full time to food getting and household tasks requiring skill
and experience. It should be emphasized that the age at which a
child begins to make important contributions to the running of the
household largely depends on the number of elder brothers and
sisters he has.

Children occasionally earn money for doing chores for relatives or outsiders living in the village. Money earned in this way
is often taken from a child if it is needed for food. On the other
hand, adult unmarried individuals living with their parents often
do not contribute their earnings to the support of the family.

All boys begin to do some hunting in the spring when they are
about twelve years old. How much they do often depends upon the
amount of assistance and encouragement they get from their fathers. Fathers are seldom observed hunting with their young sons
but there is ample opportunity for youngsters to learn basic skills
on their own as they grow up. Shooting accuracy can be achieved
by summer practice with a .22 rifle and by the constant use of

slingshots from an early age. Boys learn to throw the dragline and are usually fairly accurate with it by the time they reach the age of sixteen or seventeen. Youngsters were also observed paddling the small skin boats in the slough in springtime. Although skills must be learned with practically no direction, children have abundant opportunities to observe their elders and their interest is maintained by the vital importance of food-getting activities in the family living pattern.

The period of youth is a relatively long one at Point Hope and there is no clearly defined time limit to it. Boys are regarded as youths when they reach the age of fifteen or sixteen and begin to take on at least some of the men's work. Marriage terminates the period although young married men are often more closely associated with the unmarried youths than the adults in ideas and interests.

Unmarried youths of seventeen to twenty-five constitute, in many ways, the least well-adjusted age group. Not many of them hunt regularly, and they have a great deal of free time since they are above the age at which they are expected to do chores at home. The interests in this group are centered, for the most part, outside the village and most of them are only mildly interested in traditional village activities. A large number of young men seek employment away from the village during the summer and feel that a steady year-round job would be the answer to all their problems. Many feel that the life of a hunter at Point Hope is too much work and yet they hesitate to leave the village permanently to seek year-round employment in unfamiliar surroundings.

Most young men join the Alaska National Guard when they are seventeen, which provides them not only with a small amount of money and clothing, but also an opportunity to travel to Anchorage once a year for the two-week encampment. The trip is an excellent opportunity for young men to have a "good time," and they take full advantage of it.

Many older people are aware of the fact that young men are not learning to hunt as well as they did in the old days. Formerly, young men were taught the lore of hunting and ice conditions by the older men in the ceremonial house; now that these organizations have lost their former functions, there is no adequate substitute. The president of the village council told me that he favored the idea of having classes and demonstrations in hunting techniques and ice lore for young people in the hope that this might bring back the old custom of having younger men accompanied by older ones when out on the ice. Formerly a young man seldom

hunted by himself until he was twenty-five years of age because
of the dangers of moving ice and the necessity of becoming thoroughly familiar with ice conditions before hunting alone. Now there
is little instruction and only a few of the younger men hunt regularly, even though the introduction of the rifle and the possibility
of hunting at open leads closer to shore have made hunting safer.
A few young men say that they learned to hunt from their fathers,
but there was little evidence of that in 1956.

There appears to be a definite lack of communication between
adult men and women and their older children. They have little
in common and very little to talk about. Older men do not seem to
understand younger ones nor is there any common ground for understanding. Today, the values and standards of young men are at
least partly based on their experiences outside the village while
older people are oriented toward traditional village interests and
activities. No longer are young men growing up to carry out the
same activities and live the same kind of lives as their fathers.
This is also true to a lesser extent of young women. Two generations that do not share the same experiences and goals are bound
to find it difficult to understand each other.

Young women do not form as distinct a group as the young men,
partly because the age at which they marry is younger and also
because in recent years a larger number of girls than boys have
gone to the Bureau of Indian Affairs High School at Mt. Edgecumbe
and have not returned to the village. Young women and older school-
girls have less free time than the men because their duties in a
large family increase rather than decrease as they grow older.
Older girls share actively in all women's work, although they are
not so proficient at these tasks as one would expect considering
the early age at which they begin them.

Over the past few years, all the graduates of the eighth-grade
class at the Point Hope School have been going on to high school;
this has cut down appreciably the number of young people of both
sexes in the village. Whether they will return to the village when
they complete their education is a question that as yet cannot be
answered. If they do, the problems of adjustment to village life
will be even greater than now for that age group.

Most Point Hope boys seem to become interested in girls when
they are fifteen or sixteen years old and still in school. Apparently
there are numerous opportunities for passing "love letters" during
school hours and some boys watch carefully for opportunities to
find girls alone after school and kiss them. One boy said that his
girl would purposely wait until the other students had left the school

and then meet him in the storm shed where they would kiss two or three times. On other occasions they would go to the Wednesday evening church service, taking advantage of the darkness to kiss and talk about love to each other. Another young man said that when he was in the eighth grade, one of the favorite topics of conversation among the boys concerned the physical characteristics of certain girls that the boys had seen, or claimed to have seen, undressed. However, in describing beauty, Point Hopers generally put great emphasis on the face and say that the rest of the body does not make much difference.

Apparently premarital sex relations are not uncommon. Some young men told of having intercourse as early as sixteen and all unmarried men in the age group eighteen to twenty-five boasted of numerous conquests. Girls seem to be acquiescent, although one gets the impression that they often become involved more out of an inability to say no than because of any enjoyment on their part. As mentioned earlier, finding a secluded place for love meetings is not an easy one. One young man told of bringing girls to his parents' house at night without encountering any overt objections on their part. A few young married couples have homes of their own. These houses are regular meeting places for young people at all times, and apparently also made available for clandestine meetings. Parents appear to be dissatisfied with this state of affairs, but take no overt action and make no attempt to watch unmarried sons and daughters. The church teaches that it is wrong to have intercourse before marriage and the people know this. However, it does not have much effect on behavior.

When a child is born out of wedlock, the missionary talks to the couple involved, if the father can be determined, in an attempt to get them to marry. The priest is generally successful unless there are strong family objections. During my stay in the village, a father refused to allow his daughter to marry the father of her child because he did not think that the man could support her.

Women who have given birth to illegitimate children do not appear to be under any particular stigma, nor are the children. Most men take a joking attitude toward the situation and several older men openly teased unmarried mothers about their situation in my presence. One informant appeared to be displeased with a sister-in-law who had a child out of wedlock, while another was displeased by the sight of children his wife had given birth to before she married him.

When a small army detachment was located near Point Hope several years ago, a number of local girls became friendly with soldiers and several children resulted. Local young men were annoyed and viewed with considerable disfavor any girl that appeared to prefer soldiers to men from their own village.

Polygamy and polyandry were practiced by the Point Hope people in aboriginal times but marriages have been monogamous since the mission was founded seventy years ago. Girls marry between the ages of sixteen and twenty-five while boys are usually somewhat older. In 1956, several boys over twenty-five had not yet married. Men tend to be three or four years older than their wives. Men do not put any particular value on their prospective wives' being virgins, but there seems to be a general attitude that if a girl has been too promiscuous no one will want to marry her.

I observed no courtship patterns during my stay in the village (which is not to say they were lacking). It was very difficult to predict that a couple would eventually marry, in the absence of overt signs of friendship between particular boys and girls. Formerly, a union was arranged by the mothers of the couple, and it is possible that this occurs occasionally today. Marriage with cousins was preferred because it tended to reinforce family unity and to give the individual closer ties with persons who could help him in hunting or in times of trouble. Today, these are not considerations because the number of marriageable women in the village is small and decreasing as more girls go out to school. A man does well to find a wife at all, not to mention one who stands in the preferred relationship to him. Also, many more young men marry girls from neighboring villages than was formerly the case.

Marriages are performed by the Episcopal priest in the church, generally with relatively little ceremony. The couple moves into the home of the parents of the bride or groom, whichever has the most room. A large proportion of marriages take place after the birth of a child or after one has been conceived.

Young men often appear reluctant to marry and this is probably partly due to the relatively high degree of sexual freedom in the village. Also they do not like to give up the free life and lack of responsibility that is characteristic of unmarried youths. Since young men have seldom done much hunting prior to their marriage, and are not really equipped to be heads of families, the transition to married life is often a rather difficult one economically. Bilocal residence and large cooperative households somewhat cushion a young man's shift to heading a family but do not change his desire eventually to have a home of his own.

So-called "wife exchange," one of the most misrepresented and overpublicized aspects of Eskimo social structure, was practiced at Point Hope in the past as a practical, not an emotional arrangement, serving to draw unrelated families together for mutual support and protection, and was a recognized method of extending the family membership (Rainey, 1947, p. 242). Probably not common at any time, the last case of "wife exchange" is said to have taken place around 1940.

There have been no divorces in the village in recent years, and only one separation. The cost of a divorce in Alaska is about $200 and therefore prohibitive for most Point Hopers. Formerly, divorce, or actually separation, was fairly common before children were born, but rare afterward (Rainey, 1947, p. 243). A number of present-day families have had marital difficulties over the years, mostly due to drunkenness and prolonged absence from the village, and some of these might have ended in divorce except for the expense. Several men expressed the thought that it would be a terrible thing if their wives were unfaithful to them but were vague about what they would do under such circumstances.

The point of entry into adult status is difficult to determine because it does not always appear to be directly associated with marriage. Some young married couples retain their contacts with unmarried counterparts and share the same interests, while others immediately become interested in adult affairs and occupied with adult activities. The speed with which a young married man becomes an adult in the full sense depends largely upon the extent to which he is responsible for the welfare of his family. A young man who continues to live in a large family after he is married may be slower to take on the responsibilities of adulthood than one who sets up a household of his own and is immediately responsible for feeding himself and his wife and children. Even under the best of circumstances, marriage rarely, if ever, means complete independence for the new family. Young men are seldom experienced enough to maintain their families by their own efforts alone and depend heavily on assistance from relatives.

The early years of marriage appear to be a somewhat difficult time for women. Household chores are considerably more arduous than before marriage and added to these are the duties of child care. Often a young married woman will move in with her husband's family and may find herself somewhat dominated by her mother-in-law, who is glad to have someone to relieve her of part of her work. However, the difficulties can easily be overemphasized by a person from outside the culture. The bride is called "daughter" by her mother-in-law and, in a large measure, is treated exactly as a daughter would be. In some sense the extra work that a young married woman is sometimes called upon to perform is a part of gaining adult status and of the retirement of the parents to a less active life. As a woman grows older, has many children who in turn begin to reach the age of usefulness, she gains in prestige and position even if she continues to live with her husband's or her own parental family.

When a young married man moves in with his own or his wife's family, he becomes a functioning member of the household, contributing his skills to the common lot, mainly under the nominal direction of his father or father-in-law. At the same time he gradually acquires the techniques and skills necessary to support a family, the transition to adult responsibilities thereby being eased. If he continues to be a part of an extended family, he will take over a greater share of the responsibility of supporting its members. In some ways the activities of adult men are less varied than those of the women. Hunting consumes a large part of every day and strictly follows the pattern of the seasonal cycle. Women work long hours at home at varied tasks and with numerous interruptions of one kind or another.

The Point Hope ideal of family life, as in many other cultures, is harmonious cooperation between husband and wife. Also as in other cultures, some households are characterized by continual quarreling and disaffection between marriage partners. Much more commonly seen in Point Hope are harmonious households in which at least mutual understanding and toleration have been achieved; probably in the majority of cases there is also affection and trust between husband and wife. In harmonious households, most family activities are discussed together by a man and his wife, and for the most part they share a common social life.

An important social relationship involving adult men is the "partner" concept. Aboriginally, this term was used to identify the relationship between two individuals in different villages who were "partners" for purposes of trade. Thus, if inland people were trading with coastal people, or one coastal village trading with another, it would be advantageous for a person to have a trading partner both to trade with and to offer protection if any ill feeling between members of the two villages developed. If, for example, a Point Hope man should have sexual relations with a woman at Noatak, the child that resulted would often be considered as a "partner" with its father's other children at Point Hope. This is one way in which the intervillage partner relationships were established and the term for this relationship *(katangun)* was formerly an important one.

Today the partner concept of the type just described has nearly died out, although in recent years a few individuals continued to maintain this kind of contact in other villages. A present-day variation of the old concept is the hunting partnership within the village, the partners being persons who regularly hunt together and cooperate with each other in a variety of activities. These relationships are based entirely on friendship and mutual compatability although the partners are also often related. The partner concept signifies a strictly reciprocal relationship; if a person does something for or makes a gift to his partner, he expects help in return when he needs it. This type of partner relationship works out very well under modern employment circumstances. Two men who are partners may take turns working away from the village during the summer, one individual remaining at home to care for the dogs and do the hunting for both families.[5]

Entry to adult life was found to be gradual rather than abrupt. Likewise, the transition to old age is not clear-cut. Parents whose children are grown, married, and have moved away from home are not necessarily old by Point Hope standards. Eskimo men seem to age early in terms of appearance, but remain active until relatively advanced years. Women do not seem to be concerned by the menopause, which comes between forty and fifty; it is not a particularly important period in their lives. If there is a difference in individual reactions to the menopause, it may have a psychological basis or may reflect the presence or absence of physiological difficulties. When an individual reaches the age of sixty-five, and therefore receives a monthly old-age-assistance check, he definitely is considered "old" by the villagers.

In former times, old people were feared and suspected, because they were assumed to have a special power of influencing one's future simply by willing it. This power was attributed to all old people and was considered a great danger to children, who might become crippled or weak because of some offense against an aged person. The traditional Eskimo practice of exposing the aged to die when they had become useless was never followed at Point Hope because of this strong belief in their power (Rainey, 1947, p. 279).

Although old people are no longer feared because of presumed supernatural power, they are still respected and cared for by children and other relatives. They are able to make a positive

---

[5]For a detailed treatment of the partnership concept at Point Barrow, Alaska, see Spencer, 1959, pp. 167-77.

contribution to the household by means of the monthly old-age-assistance checks that they receive. In fact, more than one household depends heavily on the additional income brought in by a member who is over sixty-five. Most old people at Point Hope own houses which they share with a married son or daughter in return for assistance and support. In cases such as this, the old-age-assistance check is made available for the use of the entire household.

The problems of inheritance are handled loosely in the village. Old people often make their wishes known before they die. However, when this is not the case, the children get together after the death and divide the material possessions remaining. Sometimes this leads to quarrels among the surviving relatives, and if these cannot be worked out by those concerned, the village council steps in and renders a decision. Controversies involving inheritance that come to the attention of the council usually are concerned with the disposal of houses or other important items of material culture such as boats, sleds, dogs, and the like. The council hears all sides of the argument and attempts to arrive at a fair decision. All other factors being equal, the council will decide in favor of the oldest male relatives, and adopted children do not fare so well as other children in these decisions.

Although quarrels involving the inheritance of material wealth are relatively rare, there has been a tendency in recent years for old people with considerable possessions to leave wills. Various council members have encouraged this. These wills are simply a statement of how the individuals want their possessions distributed after their death and are kept in the council files. The president of the council has seen to it that the wills are properly drawn and witnessed.

In general, it seems that Point Hope people are not particularly depressed by old age unless they are in poor health. All are adequately provided for economically and most have large families to assist them in every way. Even the oldest men and women can keep themselves busy with light chores around the house, or by sitting and visiting. One old man spends most of each day seated in the store talking to whomever comes in, another is active in church work, while most elderly women still retain excellent talents as sewers. However, old people do not occupy positions of authority in the village, and those who formerly possessed great authority through their prestige as hunters or through family connections find themselves shunted aside in favor of younger more vigorous and forward-looking individuals. Point Hopers are practical people who are looking forward, not backward. Their interests are in the Point Hope of today and tomorrow, not of yesterday.

Mourning for the dead is restrained and, for the most part, private. Somewhat more grief is shown when the deceased is a child or a person in the prime of life. Ideas about death and afterlife are essentially simplified versions of those of the Church. All people who die are believed to go directly to heaven where they enjoy eternal life free from the worries and cares of this world. Living people believe that they will see their dead relatives in the other world. However, death and the afterlife are not common subjects for conversation and people accept what they read in the Bible and hear in church, perhaps without a great deal of conviction, but at the same time without feeling that it is necessary to discuss the pros and cons of the subject.

When a person is dying, members of his family send for the priest in the hope that communion may be administered. Relatives begin to arrive when death is thought to be near and remain after it has taken place. Friends may also call at the house of the deceased at this time and there is apt to be some show of emotion on the part of close relatives. The priest or a lay reader comes after the death and there is talk on religious subjects and perhaps some reading from the Bible.

It is the custom to clothe the body entirely in white before placing it in the coffin. The body of an adult is sometimes wrapped in a shroud of white cloth. A white flannel shirt and pants are often sewn by relatives for a deceased boy or man. For babies, a little white dress is adequate, with white socks and a small white cap with some kind of ornamentation. All dead persons wear white canvas gloves obtained at the store.

The coffin is constructed by relatives from lumber purchased from the store, and is built as soon as possible after death, usually in the house of the deceased. The inside of the coffin is lined with white cloth and blankets are sometimes placed over the corpse. The outside of the coffin is covered with white oilcloth, and a cloth cross or artificial flowers cut from cloth arranged in the form of a cross are fastened on the cover of the coffin at its head.

Funeral services take place as soon after death as is convenient for the relatives of the deceased. The service for the dead is read in church and the coffin is then placed on a sled and pulled out to the cemetery, located about one-half mile northeast of the village. Funerals are not attended by many people besides close relatives of the deceased; the funerals of very old people are better attended than others. When the funeral party arrives at the cemetery, the priest reads the burial service, the coffin is lowered into the grave, and a little gravel is tossed in before the grave is filled. Occasionally a hymn is sung. When deaths occur during the winter, the coffin is buried temporarily in a snow bank at the cemetery until graves can be dug in the late spring. When this is the case, only part of the burial service is read, the rest being read at the time of the actual interment.

During the nineteenth century, the dead were placed on whalebone scaffolds erected in the vicinity of the village. Around 1910, the Church was successful in persuading the people to take down the scaffolds and to use the bones, mostly whale ribs, to enclose an area to be used as a cemetery. The earliest graves date from about 1914. Graves are often marked with a simple wooden cross with the name of the deceased and the date of death cut on it. Some are more elaborate with wooden fences built around the grave and religious mottoes added to the more personal information. On the other hand, quite a few graves are completely unmarked. Relatives of deceased persons visit the cemetery occasionally and sometimes place artificial wreaths on the graves or small bunches of tundra flowers gathered during the summer. Point Hope people are extremely anxious to be buried in the village cemetery and have a fear of dying away from home. Several years ago a man died of tuberculosis in the hospital at Sitka. His wife wanted very much for his body to be returned to the village and arrangements were made, at considerable expense, for it to be brought on the *North Star* in the fall.

Remembrances of dead relatives and photographs of deceased family members often occupy an important position in the home. One man wears a white shirt belonging to his dead brother every Christmas Day, while a woman has a special pair of skin boots that her newest baby always wears for baptism. This was the last pair of boots softened (by chewing) by her husband's cousin (and brother's fiancee) before she was killed in an airplane crash three years ago. A young man whose wife died in the hospital at Tacoma wore her jewelry after it was returned to him and had a ring with her picture in it.

Villagers could remember only one suicide in the village but the early mission records list another as having taken place about fifty years ago. This is a low figure compared with other villages in Alaska. Nothing definite could be learned concerning the causes of the two suicides.

7

SOCIAL STRUCTURE
AND
COMMUNITY LIFE

THE TERM *Eskimo* has been used to designate a type in all important kinship studies and has recently been redefined by Murdock in his comprehensive kinship study, *Social Structure*. Murdock identifies six types of kinship terminology: Eskimo, Hawaiian, Iroquois, Sudanese, Omaha, and Crow (Murdock, 1949, pp. 223-24). His definition of the Eskimo type refers to a specific cross-cousin terminology; father's sister's daughters and mother's brother's daughters are called by the same terms as those used for parallel cousins but are terminologically differentiated from sisters (Murdock, 1949, p. 223). The more specific features of Murdock's classification follow:

Eskimo cousin terms
No exogamous unilinear kin groups

Theoretically, the following features are also characteristic:

Monogamy
Independent nuclear families
Lineal terms for aunts and nieces
Bilateral extension of incest taboos
Frequent presence of such bilateral kin groups as kindreds and
demes

(Murdock, 1949, pp. 226-27).

The kinship terms of the Point Hope Eskimo can be summarized as follows:

Second ascending generation grouped by sex with two terms used.
Second descending generation grouped by sex with two terms used.
Brother and sister terms are: older brother, younger brother, older sister, younger sister.
The same term is used for father's brother and mother's brother, but the term is different from that used for father.
The same term is used for father's sister and mother's sister, but the term is different from that used for mother.

Parallel-cousin terms are as follows: one term for father's brother's child and a different one for mother's sister's child. Cross-cousin terms: like terms.

Parallel- and cross-cousin terms differ from each other.

It will be immediately apparent that the Point Hope system does not show the Eskimo type of cousin terminology as described by Murdock. Rather it employs cousin terms he has defined as Iroquoian. This seems to indicate that among the various groups of Eskimos there is considerably greater variation in kin terms, and in social structure in general for that matter, than Murdock was aware of at the time he formulated his type. Murdock's Eskimo kin type is based entirely on two groups of Eskimos from the eastern Arctic, the Copper Eskimo from the central Canadian Arctic, and the Angmagssalik of Greenland. Only in recent years have data been collected on Alaskan Eskimo kinship systems, and it seems likely that as information accumulates, considerable variation in kin terms will be recognized. A notable degree of subcultural diversity exists through the Eskimo area and it is thus virtually impossible to refer to any regionally developed social structure as representative of Eskimos in general (see Giddings, 1952b, and Hughes, 1958).

Point Hope social structure is further characterized by preferred parallel- or cross-cousin marriage, bilateral descent, and bilocal residence. The preference for cousin marriage, stronger formerly than it is today, is, as previously mentioned, largely defeated by the relatively small number of marriageable women in the village.

Although bilocal residence is characteristic of the village social structure and inherent in the extended family system that was once an integral part of the social system, neolocal residence is preferred and is the ideal of most young married people. The problem of housing is a difficult one. Although young married couples express a desire eventually to have a home of their own, from a financial standpoint this is virtually impossible. Occasionally the death of relatives provides a young couple with a house much sooner than they would otherwise obtain one. A young married couple normally lives with the side of the family that is best equipped to receive them. Occasionally they alternate, spending part of their time with each set of relatives.

The joking relationship, a form of culturally patterned behavior toward relatives, is very loose and ill-defined in the village today. An individual jokes with his cousins, either cross or parallel, providing he wishes to have that kind of relationship with them. There is no obligation to indulge in joking or horseplay with cousins, but frequently individuals so related will make jokes at each other's expense. Some people also maintain a sort of joking relationship with affinal relatives, but only if they are already friendly with them before marriage. A person need not feel obliged to enter into such a relationship simply because he becomes related to a person through marriage. An individual does not normally joke or indulge in horseplay with close consanguineal kin. An attitude of respect should be shown at all times toward one's parents, grandparents, brothers, and sisters. However, this seems to be an ideal pattern and, especially today, does not hold true in all cases. Cases of bitter disagreements, even resulting in fighting, between children and parents have been reported in the village, although they are probably very rare. However, I witnessed a number of cases of severe impudence of older children to their parents. Certain affinal kin, particularly mothers-in-law and fathers-in-law, are shown respect at all times, but are not avoided.

An unusual type of relationship is that existing between unrelated children of two married people. The term for this relationship is *katangun,* and people so related have the option of joking with one another. Formerly this term had more significance than it does today because it was also used to designate the relationship between a man or woman's legitimate and illegitimate children. It thus would apply to children resulting from wife exchange.

Murdock has postulated that with the Eskimo type of kinship terminology one can expect to find no exogamous unilinear kin groups. Point Hope is a community that is characterized for the most part by village endogamy and is not segmented by unilinear consanguineal groupings of kinsmen. Because of the fact that local endogamy is prevalent, the inhabitants are necessarily related to one another through intermarriage though they are not always able to trace the exact kinship connections. Within the community the only social structuring is into families and, except for family ties, the strongest sense of identification is with the community as a whole. Murdock refers to this type of grouping as a *deme* (Murdock, 1949, p. 63).

The extended family group, once the basis of social structure, has long since been replaced by relatively small conjugal units, usually composed of a man, his wife, their children, and perhaps one or two dependent relatives. Rainey has pointed out that once open feuds disappeared, the need for the powerful combined families that once characterized Point Hope social structure was no longer urgent (Rainey, 1947, p. 240).

When young couples can afford to build their own house, they may choose to construct it in close proximity to the home of the older relatives with whom they once lived; thus certain areas of the village are associated with particular expanded families. Men related by blood or marriage tend to hunt together and they help each other when hunting conditions have been bad. The sharing of equipment among related people is also prevalent. Apparently the existing system of small conjugal families occupying their own dwellings has been in existence for a considerable length of time. In 1940, Rainey was unable to get much information even from the oldest people about the old extended family groups.

Within the typical family certain routines and habits are characteristic. For example, the family often rises about 7:30 or 8:00 A. M. Breakfast is served so that the children can be at school by 9:00, lunchtime is around noon, and the evening meal is eaten when the man of the house returns from hunting. These hours vary somewhat from family to family, and in summer, when the days are long, family sleeping patterns are irregular. The family sleeps in one or two beds, with older children occasionally unrolling sleeping bags on the floor. A mother often sleeps with her arms around her infant so that she will be easily awakened by any movements or noise that he makes.

The general weekly routine is somewhat as follows: On Sunday most families attend the church service which begins at 11:00 A. M. The children stay afterward for Sunday school. Since few people do any kind of work on Sunday, most of the rest of the day is spent in relaxation or visiting. Those who do not attend church usually sleep late. A large meal is eaten late in the afternoon and a lighter one before retiring at night. Sunday evening is the time for visiting and many families entertain couples for card playing, or just talking, or perhaps they go to a neighbor's home themselves. A man and his wife go visiting together or separately. Children and young unmarried men and women visit here and there on Sunday nights quite as they do every other night. Families never retire early, but Sunday evening card games or visits often do not break up until 2:00 or 3:00 o'clock in the morning.

On weekdays, particularly during the winter, the men go out to hunt shortly after it gets light and remain away from home most of the daylight hours. Women busy themselves with household chores and the care of infants until the school children return at noon, when a light lunch is prepared. The main housework is cleaning the house, washing dishes and clothes, and tending the fire. Other chores include sewing, scraping skins, and making trips to the store for groceries. Women do not seem to visit a great deal during

the day, although they may take small children out for a while and
stop to visit someone. Women often spend considerable time at the
store during the day, where they meet their friends and exchange
news and gossip about village events.

When the men return from hunting they may have certain chores
to do. As noted earlier, a man's wife helps him unharness his dogs,
just as she has helped to harness them in the morning. After that
he prepares the dog food and feeds the dogs. If he has been successful, he brings the game into the storm shed and perhaps takes
a seal into the house to thaw preparatory to its being skinned by
his wife the following day. The main meal of the day is served
shortly after the men return from hunting. In the spring and summer when there is almost total daylight, eating schedules vary
considerably because the hours of hunting and other activities are
quite irregular; the various members of the family take their meals
whenever they are at home and happen to be hungry. Children return from school between 4:00 P. M. and 5:30 or 6:00 P. M., and
may or may not be present when the family meals are eaten. If
not, they help themselves to whatever is left.

Family activities on weekdays are much the same throughout
the week. There is a church service on Wednesday evening, which
many attend. National Guard drills, village movies at the schoolhouse, as well as the meetings of various village organizations
help to fill weekday evenings. In fact, it is often difficult to find
an evening during the week when some activity is not scheduled.

In aboriginal times, each person in the village was a member
of one of the six or seven ceremonial organizations of the village.
Children became members of their father's organization, but a
girl assumed membership in her husband's when she married. Occasionally a young person might join the organization of his namesake if the latter so desired. Normally a man remained a member
of the same organization all his life, but occasionally changes were
made, particularly if unfriendly relations between fellow organization members developed. One villager belonged to his maternal
grandfather's organization rather than his father's because his
grandfather reared him after his father died.

Although the organizations were essentially ceremonial, they
also had considerable social significance. Praise or censorship
of a person's actions as expressed by fellow members undoubtedly
served as a powerful force for social control. Children were taught
proper social behavior by the old men during the ceremonies. Since
the organization's structure was essentially a men's house, it was
there that the men and boys worked on hunting equipment, re-

paired boats, and listened to old stories told by the older men. In
this way the folklore and behavior patterns of the group were trans-
mitted from generation to generation (Rainey, 1947, p. 242).

Today there is very little left of the organizations. Only two remain and these are significant only in so far as they affect the pat-
terning of some of the ceremonial activities performed at Christmas and the feast at the end of the whaling season. Except at these
times, ceremonial affiliation seems to have meaning only as a remembered link with the past. No one but perhaps the four or five
oldest men in the village remembers anything about the activities
of the ceremonial organizations as they used to be carried out.

In 1920 the Episcopal Church organized a village council to control the local affairs of the village, and in 1940, when the village
became chartered as a corporation of the United States, the council
came under the jurisdiction of the Alaska Native Service of the Bureau of Indian Affairs. In 1956 the Point Hope Village Council consisted of eleven members elected for three-year terms. Four are
elected on each of two years and three the third year. Recently a
change was made in the bylaws permitting the election of women.
Apparently no woman has ever run for the council, although occasionally women with secretarial training have been admitted to
meetings for the purpose of recording the minutes. The council has
a president, vice-president, secretary, treasurer, and marshal.
Also there are a film manager who is in charge of ordering and
returning the weekly movies sponsored by the council, one or more
recreational officers who are in charge of planning programs at
Christmas and Thanksgiving, a property officer who is in charge
of various properties belonging to council, and an auditor who
makes periodic checks on store business.

The council advises on many aspects of village life. Much of its
time is taken up with store business, but it is also in charge of all
civic functions and concerns itself with various civic improvements,
North Star unloading, property settlements, and minor quarrels
between individuals or families that cannot be settled by the people
involved. Recently the council has become interested in civic improvements and backed a 2 per cent sales tax that, in 1956, had
been in effect for more than two years. Money collected in this
way has been used to improve the water system and to provide for
emergencies. During 1955-56, council money was used to buy vitamin pills for preschool children and penicillin for the school clinic
when its supply became depleted. Some council members think of
Point Hope as a tourist attraction, and in that connection are interested in preserving the old songs and stories on tape recordings

so that younger people may learn them. The council president feels that many tourists will come to the village when the present airstrip is enlarged, and he would like to see a ceremonial house reconstructed so that dances might be held there as a tourist attraction.

The council acts also as a rule-making and law-enforcing body although it has no power to enforce its rulings. If individuals lodge complaints against others, these are handled by the council. Cases of public drunkenness and various other misdemeanors are punished by fines. The council has the power to shoot dogs that are not tied and can levy a fine against individuals who do not haul dead dogs out on the ice. Teachers occasionally bring misbehavior of children to the attention of the council, which in turn calls on the parents and discusses the matter with them. The council is surprisingly effective as an enforcement agency. The pressures of public opinion, together with the prestige of the council members, are important factors in encouraging compliance with village rules and regulations. The United States Marshal at Nome has jurisdiction over the Point Hope area and he may come to the village to arrest individuals who have committed crimes against the American legal system. Cases of this kind, which are relatively few, are handled with the cooperation of the village council.

The council president presides at the meetings and conclusions are reached after long discussions. Each councilman has his say and occasionally a formal vote is taken. However, more frequently everyone is in agreement by the time a matter has been fully discussed. If the presence of villagers is needed during the course of a meeting, the council marshal is sent to get them. The decisions reached by the council are almost always based on precedent and the group is loath to put aside any old custom. The most persuasive argument that can be offered in favor of any subject is to say that that is the way it has been done in the past. In all cases where the council must take disciplinary action, there is an attempt to avoid open conflict and the decisions always reflect the desire to maintain peace and order in the village.

The method by which the council reaches a decision in a matter involving conflict of interest is shown well in the minutes of a meeting held on April 5, 1950, reproduced here in their entirety:

> The Point Hope Council meeting was held at the schoolhouse. Those present were: [members listed].
>
> Daniel L., Secretary, was appointed by President Roy V. to act as chairman in the case of Andrew F. Andrew caught a walrus that sunk. After two days it was afloat and discovered by Carl T., Nicholas H.,

Panniluke, and John L. Daniel L. asked the members what their opinion
was on the matter.

Moses said that a long time ago, Dives sunk a walrus at the point in the
spring. Moses knew of it. After a couple of days, it came to the surface
and was afloat. Moses, Alec M. and Kirk O. were there. They hooked it
and notified the owner. The owner of the walrus divided the meat equally
among them and gave one tusk to Kirk and Alec for hooking it.

Daniel ordered Patrick to get Andrew F., the owner of the walrus. Patrick, our native council marshal, came with Andrew F.

The acting chairman asked Andrew F. what his opinion was. He said that
when he went down on the ice he expected to catch a seal and to his surprise a walrus popped up. He thought it was a whale at first. He shot it
first along the front and with the next shot it went down. After a little
while it came up again. He said he shot it again in the head. The last shot
was in the head and it sank with the last shot. He waited for a long time
and shot a seal later and came home. The next day he said he went down
again. He met Panniluke, Augustus, Billy, and Al. He told Panniluke
where he sank it. The next day he wasn't feeling too well so he didn't go
down. The following evening Andrew heard Carl T., Panniluke, and Nicholas had found the walrus. He waited to be notified by the fellows about the
walrus. The next night he went over to see Carl himself. He asked Carl
if he had found the walrus. Carl said yes. He said he didn't know a thing
about it until Panniluke told him. Andrew added that he told Nicholas about
the walrus that he sunk the day before it came to the surface. Nicholas
knew about it all the time and did not tell Carl T. about it. Andrew questioned Panniluke. Panniluke said that he would rather hear about it from
the councilmen.

After that Andrew went over to President V. and asked for his opinion.
Roy said so far as he could see, the man that killed the animal is always
owner. Regardless of the species of the animal. Roy ordered him to see
Vice-President Eebrulik R. and got the same answer.

Jakie suggested that if the owner of the walrus is known, and the walrus
is found in the same place, it is the custom among the Eskimos that the
head of a walrus belongs to the owner. He added that one time he went
out hunting and came to a lead. He found a dead walrus there. He got the
help of Rex and Jacob. They dragged it up on the pack ice and divided
it. Later Rueben came along and said he was the owner of the walrus.
Rueben received half of the walrus up to the flippers. Jakie added that
as far as he understood, the head of the walrus belonged to Andrew and
also some share of the meat. That was only a suggestion.

Matt said that when the owner of the animal is known, it always belongs
to the owner. He also added that Andrew was the only one that sunk the
walrus.

Bob said that it is always better to do right. He said that he agreed with
what Jakie said. When the owner is known, it rightfully belongs to the
man that killed the animal.

Andrew said that he wanted the tusks and some share of the meat divided
equally among the others.

Patrick said Jakie's suggestion about the walrus is the thing to follow.

Marshal Patrick came in with Carl, Panniluke, and John L. Nicholas was unable to come.

The acting chairman questioned Carl T. about the walrus that Andrew killed. He said that he would do whatever the Council decided to do. At that time Carl T. did not know about it. He thought he found the walrus that died by itself.

Panniluke said whatever they decided would be all right. He said he was the last one to be there.

Jakie repeated his speech about what he had done before and suggested that they do the same thing.

Bob questioned Carl T. about giving up the tusks to Andrew and the share of the meat. Carl said he would like to have a share of the tusks because he found it.

Donald asked Panniluke who might have sunk the walrus. Panniluke answered Andrew.

Donald asked again how he would feel if he sunk a walrus and nothing was left for him. He said he would have nothing to do with it because he didn't help and wasn't there.

Donald asked Andrew what he thought of receiving the tusks, what he would do or give Carl who found it. Andrew said that if he received the tusks, he would give Carl whatever he desired.

Jakie said it is a custom that in the winter any animal that is identified goes to the owner and in the summer people that do hunting for dead walrus along the beach and found any, got that walrus. Matt said the same thing as Jakie. They are following the rules that were passed down from our ancestors. Anybody could tell that this was Andrew's walrus.

Daniel asked Carl if he would give the tusks to Andrew and let him give Carl what he desires. Carl said it was alright with him.

Patrick said that the majority of the Council wanted to let Andrew have the tusks. The same thing applies with foxes caught in traps. When anybody found the foxes, they always go to the owner. In this case it happened to be Herbert. He promised him $5 if he would give the fox to him. When he turned it over to the store he gave him $2.50. He complained to David and did not receive any more than $2.50. It is always the owner that takes charge of any animal killed.

Andrew will give Carl T. $3 out of that walrus tusk. Meeting was adjourned at 12:25 A.M.

Signed Daniel L.

The council is very effective in dealing with immediate problems similar to the one just described but considerably less successful in handling long-range problems. Often good ideas are brought up and discussed at the meetings and approved. However, nothing is done about them and they tend to die a natural death.

At one time the yearly election of council members was controlled by a few leading men in the village whose families voted as they were told. At the time when the Point Hope Trading Company, a village-owned store, was in existence, large stockholders were influential and the same individual was president of the council for many years because he was the largest stockholder (Rainey, 1947, p. 282). Today, every adult appears to have an equal voice in the election. In recent years the election procedure has consisted of the council nominating two candidates for each position that is up for election. These two names are placed on a ballot with a blank place where the voter can write in any candidate that he wishes. However, it is generally conceded that a write-in candidate has little or no chance of being elected. Thus, the council does have some control over who runs for office and the elected man need not necessarily be the choice of the people. While I was in the village a new election procedure was tried. The council listed four candidates for each office and a "primary" was held at which two were eliminated. Then at the election, held always during Christmas week in the schoolhouse, the people chose one man to fill each position.

The village council is made up mostly of middle-aged and younger men. There are several old men who have been members ever since the incorporation of the village but their number is decreasing as old people do not have public support for positions of authority. Although middle-aged men still predominate, there is a tendency for younger men to work their way onto the council and at the 1956 election a thirty-five-year-old progressive was elected president. Individuals such as he have been responsible for the revised election procedure, sales tax, and other progressive measures. Although a certain element of the village is distrustful of rapid change, nearly everyone is aware of the value of having young councilmen who speak good English and are familiar with the white man's ways. It is no coincidence, perhaps, that the present council president is also the maintenance employee at the school and thus the go-between through which Eskimo-schoolteacher and Eskimo-government relations pass.

Among the other formally organized groups at Point Hope, the village Parent Teachers Association is the most active. This organization was formed about 1950 by the schoolteachers and meets regularly to discuss problems of mutual interest to the village and the school. The P. T. A. is in charge of the school nutrition program and the women take turns in baking bread and preparing the hot breakfast that is served to the school children. The organization elects a president, vice-president, secretary, and treasurer. While I was in the village the P. T. A. sponsored a carnival which netted approximately $90.00 for the group and a clothes auction at which over \$100 was taken in. Some of the money was used for presents for graduating eighth-graders but the group still had a large amount in the treasury. Rapport between the schoolteachers and the P. T. A. is good even though the American concept of what a P. T. A. is supposed to be seems to be lacking.

The Mothers' Club is a group that was first organized in 1952 by a public health nurse who was resident in the village for a brief period. It seems to be a sort of extension of the Women's Club that the Church has sponsored from time to time. The group meets occasionally to sew and talk but has never been very active. It is interesting to note that the schoolteachers several years ago attempted to abolish the Mothers' Club by merging it with the newly formed P. T. A. It is said that the latter organization was started because the teachers wanted a group through which they could attempt to run the village. At any rate, the Mothers' Club has continued. Although they meet very seldom, the money in the treasury is used as a loan fund by villagers who are temporarily in need. The Mothers' Club has occasionally cooperated with the Women's Health Council on village health projects.

The Point Hope Eskimos have been extensively exposed to European and American culture since the latter part of the nineteenth century when the North Pacific whaling fleet was active in Arctic waters. In this relatively short period of time, they have become familiar with the technical aspects of American culture and have widened their world view considerably. At the same time, their most intimate extracommunity relationships continue to be with the villages in the immediate region although, for a variety of reasons, a widened interest in the larger cities of Alaska and in life in the rest of the United States is present, too.

One of the most obvious indications of the impact of the outside world is the well-developed concept of time. Almost every adult person in the village owns a wrist watch and most homes have alarm clocks. Numerous activities in the village reinforce the awareness of time. School children must arrive at school at a definite time, have a specified lunch period, and are dismissed at a definite time. The arrival of the thrice-weekly plane, while never completely predictable, is always expected within a certain time period and people look at their watches and make comments to the effect that it should be appearing soon. Church services are held according to a definite schedule, as are most community activities. The village store is open for a specified number of hours each day. Work outside the village in such places as Kotzebue and

Fairbanks also helps to familiarize people with time schedules. Those who have radios know that certain programs start at certain times and they set their watches and clocks accordingly.

The Point Hopers are considerably more mobile than their isolated location might suggest, and probably more so today than in aboriginal times in spite of the high cost of air transportation. People talk of Kivalina and Point Lay as places that they have often visited and where they have many friends and relatives. Also Point Barrow and Wainwright are fairly well known because some have been there, and because the *North Star* stops at these towns before arriving at Point Hope; everyone follows the progress of the *North Star* either with his own radio or by asking others. Noatak is familiar as a stop that the airplane makes before arriving at Point Hope.

Kotzebue is the best known village, not only because it is the trading center and source of the mail planes, but also because everyone leaving the village to go to work, to school, or to the hospital passes through the town. When Point Hopers are in Kotzebue they always meet many people they know. Most of them have relatives living there; six families have moved to Kotzebue from Point Hope in the past ten years. The Episcopal Church in Kotzebue is a focal point for all visiting Point Hopers and it is not unusual for individuals who seldom go to church at home to attend regularly when in Kotzebue. The church service is something that is familiar to them and attendance gives them an opportunity to meet and visit with friends and relatives from home.

Fairbanks and Anchorage are the two large cities that have most meaning for the villagers. Fairbanks is familiar because many men go there to work every summer and there are two Point Hope families living there. I found that talk about places of mutual familiarity in Fairbanks was one of the best conversation devices when I first arrived in the village. Anchorage is less well known, being familiar only to those men who have attended National Guard encampments there or visited the city while in the army, either recently or during the war. Nome and Mt. Edgecumbe have been visited by some villagers. The National Guard men pass through Nome on their way to the yearly encampment at Anchorage while Mt. Edgecumbe is familiar as the location of the Bureau of Indian Affairs hospital and high school.

Curiosity about what is going on in the outside world is rare at Point Hope. Although radios are extensively owned, very seldom do people listen to anything except music and variety shows. Two or three persons subscribe to popular magazines such as *Life*,

Look, Newsweek, and *Time,* and can discuss national and international affairs with a reasonable degree of comprehension. Most people, however, have only the haziest idea of what is going on in the world, because of the limitations of their experience and the low level of their reading ability. Even the most literate individuals find reading a slow and painful process, and it is little wonder that people are much more interested in the pictures in magazines and books than they are in the written material. Everyone, however, is aware of the fact that the United States is having difficulty with the Russians and therefore the Russians are considered evil.

A voting precinct was established at Point Hope in 1945 and the villagers have since had the opportunity to vote in territorial (now state) and national elections. For reasons that are not entirely clear the village vote is overwhelmingly Democratic, and there is considerable interest in voting in spite of a general lack of understanding of the issues involved. Most of those eligible vote in every election as do a few who are presumably not eligible by reason of inability to read and write English. There are always three poll-watchers, a Democrat, a Republican, and an independent. One person jokingly told me that there would probably be no Republicans in the village were it not for the watcher's fee. Although elections have been carried on for a number of years, they do not seem to have stimulated a great deal of interest in territorial and state politics. The second Alaskan political division was occasionally represented in the territorial legislature by Eskimos and these made a special effort to get the village vote. Point Hopers seem to be more suspicious of Eskimo candidates for office than they are of whites.

The Alaska National Guard is represented by a detachment at Point Hope consisting of approximately forty men ranging in age from seventeen to over fifty. Guard members drill in the National Guard building a total of forty-eight times during the year at a rate of pay varying according to rank. The money payment to the members is a negligible factor in village economics, but the men also are issued clothing and rifles. It is the two-week encampment in Anchorage that attracts most recruits. Interest pales during the drills held in the village but nearly all Guard members seem to enjoy the training period even though they have little free time while in camp. However some do not care for the Anchorage trips and drop out at the end of their first three-year enlistment. The local National Guard unit is commanded by an army veteran of six years' service who holds the rank of Master Sergeant in the Guard.

It is curious that this man, who is highly regarded as a commanding officer, is completely devoid of anything resembling the leadership qualities that are respected in the village. He is without authority or prestige outside his position with the National Guard.

Not more than one-half dozen Point Hope men were drafted for military service during World War II because of high incidence of tuberculosis. Of those who did go, two stayed in the army and have received various assignments in the United States. None saw action although several were stationed in the Aleutians at the time of the Japanese attacks in that area. Army experience has had a broadening effect on those who served in that they speak better English and are, for the most part, more acculturated.

In spite of the increased employment opportunities throughout Alaska in the past few years, there has been no extensive movement away from Point Hope. This is in marked contrast to many other Alaskan villages and reflects the close identification that Point Hopers have with their village, as well as the continued importance of the subsistence economy. Only four families left between 1950 and 1956, and one has since returned. The remaining three families, resident in Kotzebue, are presumably there because of more favorable employment opportunities. Five women have left over a similar time period, are married to white men, and live in various Alaskan cities. Two Point Hope families have been living in Fairbanks for many years and there are several persons in other states, mostly women who are married to white men.

Since 1954, an increasing number of young people have left to attend high school at Mt. Edgecumbe. The trades taught in the Bureau of Indian Affairs school are not those which can be practiced in the village and it thus seems probable that more and more young people, having once made the break with village life, will seek steady employment in other places. Young men can return and become hunters, but young women trained as practical nurses or secretaries will find homecoming a return to dull routine without hope of employment, and to a life devoid of the refinements with which they have become familiar. It is little wonder, then, that some young women aspire to marry white men and to live permanently away from the village.

Nevertheless, as a rule Point Hope people feel very strongly about their village and are extremely happy to return after extended absences. Men who obtain seasonal employment away from the village usually leave their families behind and have worries about their welfare added to whatever homesickness they may feel.

In spite of the extensive military construction going on in northwest Alaska at the present time, Point Hope has had little direct connection with military and construction personnel. In 1952, the army established a small camp about one mile east of the village which was manned for two years and then shut down, presumably because it was difficult to supply. The commanding officers at this camp seemed to have been strongly impressed with the desirability of getting along in the village and men who became involved with village girls were transferred. One man told me that "the unmarried girls surely had a good time" but this is probably an exaggeration. The army men seem to have been particularly sensitive about being taken advantage of by the villagers. At one point, when they thought they were being overcharged for skin boots and other local products, the commanding officer threatened to stop the free movies and other services that the military was providing for the villagers. All in all, the people appear to have liked the army men and one hears many regrets that they are now gone.[6]

Sometime after 1930, at the time when the Point Hope parish hall was constructed, the missionary suggested that a feast and general entertainment be held on Thanksgiving Day. Over the years this has become an important social event in the village, second only to the ceremonies held at the Christmas season.

Thanksgiving Day festivities begin with a celebration of Holy Communion, and early in the afternoon people begin to gather in the parish hall, sitting around the walls on the floor and on benches. The seating for the feast is always by families, and certain strongly knit families make an impressive gathering with as many as four generations seated together. If a family is not close, its seating may be broken up into residential units.

The feast begins late in the afternoon after most of the people have arrived. Those bringing food take their contributions to the stage at one end of the building where members of the council and others in charge of preparations receive it. The president of the village council opens the festivities with a short speech about Thanksgiving, and if he happens to be running for re-election at Christmas time he may include a discussion of accomplishments in the village during the three years of his presidency. Following this speech, the names of those who are to serve as waiters are announced. Following a prayer by the missionary, the waiters take

---

[6]For a more detailed consideration of Point Hope's relations with the outside world, see VanStone, 1958c.

Plate V-A. Christmas Week Activities

Boys foot race

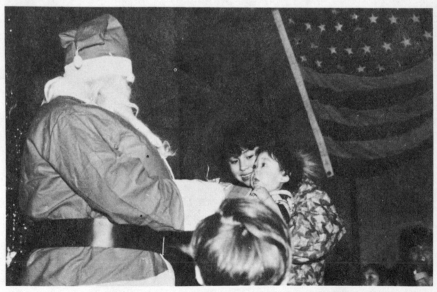

A gift from Santa Claus

Plate V-B. Christmas Week Activities

The Nativity play

Local talent

large containers of food around the room, stopping to serve everyone. Each family brings its own eating and drinking utensils. At
the Thanksgiving feast in 1955, the following items of food were
served in the order listed:
  rice and raisins
  pilot bread (a large quantity for each person)
  graham crackers
  white bread
  frozen caribou meat
  frozen black whale *muktuk*
  frozen whale meat
  frozen *ugruk* meat
  stewed dried apples with raisins
  vegetable soup with macaroni
  chocolate cake (provided by the schoolteachers)
  jello (three kinds)
  coffee, tea, milk
There is much more food than can be eaten at the time and almost
everyone takes some home. The waiters and council members eat
after everyone else has finished.

Following the meal, a series of games is held for children of
various ages. While these are going on three men prepare the
drums for a dance. The typical Eskimo tambourine with bone handle
and hardwood frame is used. The drumhead is made from the outer
covering of a whale's liver. An Eskimo dance is a traditional feature of the Thanksgiving festivities and is usually continued until
shortly after midnight, when a prayer by the missionary brings
the day's activities to a close.

In aboriginal times, a series of games, dances, and feasts was
held in the ceremonial houses during the autumn. Many of these
were directly related to whaling and in all of them the captains
played the leading part (Rainey, 1947, pp. 245-53). Today, what
remain of these festivities, together with more recent innovations,
take place during Christmas week, the high point of modern Point
Hope ceremonial life.

The activities of Christmas week apparently vary considerably
from year to year although there are certain stable features. The
school always presents a program. Other parts of the week-long
activities are in the charge of the village council. Preparations begin well in advance of Christmas because new skin boots must be
made and new clothes prepared as well, if at all possible. Women
work hard at sewing and sometimes are up all night on Christmas
Eve in an attempt to get everything finished for the big day.

The mission always has a carol service on Christmas Eve and there is a celebration of the Holy Communion on Christmas morning. On the afternoon of that day is a feast held in the parish hall which is very similar to the one at Thanksgiving. The highlight of the Christmas Day events is the appearance of Santa Claus, portrayed by someone chosen by the council, followed by a great sledload of gifts. The mission gives a present to everyone in the village and the school usually provides gifts for all the school-age children. In addition, many individuals exchange presents.

The school program is given on either Christmas Eve or Christmas night. It includes a Nativity play, songs, individual recitations, and other activities by the school children. Christmas is a time of great excitement for the children. They look forward with eager anticipation to the various activities and work hard at learning their parts for the Christmas program. Many children talk of hanging their stockings on Christmas Eve and finding them filled with toys and candy the next morning. Parents provide new clothes for their children on Christmas if they can possibly afford to do so.

Each afternoon during Christmas week the villagers gather in the parish hall for activities that usually last until midnight. At least two evenings are devoted to a series of individual contests of strength between members of two teams chosen by the council members in charge of entertainment. The contestants are seated on the floor, one team on each side of the room. One man goes to the center and is successively challenged by men from the other side until he is beaten, in which case the winner stays in the center until he, in turn, is defeated. The contests include finger pull, arm pull, and pulling on a broom handle. The performances involve demonstrations as well as contests. A person on one team may choose to perform an athletic feat such as walking on his hands, jumping from a push-up position, or jumping to touch an object suspended at a given height above the floor. Each team tries to present some test of strength or acrobatic feat at which one of its members is particularly skilled. After these games have been in progress for a couple of days, one team is declared the winner and receives a carton of cigarettes or some other prize. These games are similar to the series of competitive games of endurance and skill that were once performed in the ceremonial houses during the autumn. In the old days the ceremonial organizations competed against one another, and the games are said to have continued for five days and nights with the men and boys moving from one ceremonial house to the other with the fortune of the games (Rainey, 1947, p. 245).

Plate VI-A. Christmas Week Activities

Bringing the muktuk *for* Kakumisaq

A test of strength

Plate VI-B. Christmas Week Activities

Cutting muktuk

The entire village in the parish hall

Perhaps the high point of the Christmas week activities is the reciprocal ceremonial feast which takes place every year beginning in the early afternoon and lasting until late at night. For the purpose of this event, the parish hall is divided by a curtain as shown in the accompanying diagram (Fig. 3). The *Qagmaktoq* members seat themselves as shown in the diagram while members of the *Ungasiksikaq* organization bring food which is handed through an opening in the curtain and received by two *Qagmaktoq* who place it in the middle of the room. Whaleskin is brought spitted on sticks which are called *kakumisaq*. The ceremony is known by this name. After the food has been received it is prepared by a number of *Qagmaktoq* waiters who then pass it around to the people as at any other feast.

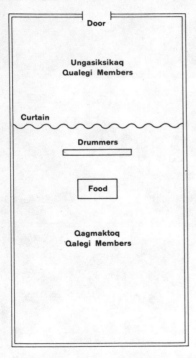

Figure 3.

Arrangement of the parish hall

for the *Kakumisaq* ceremony

While the *Qagmaktoq* members are eating, members of *Ungasiksikaq* go to their homes and get the presents that are to be distributed. As they return to the parish hall, they assemble behind the curtain waiting for *Qagmaktoq* to finish eating. When all the food has been cleared away, *Qagmaktoq* drummers seat themselves in front of the curtain, leaving a place for the dancing, and begin to drum. While this first drumming is going on, the "joy shout" comes from behind the curtain so that *Qagmaktoq* will know that *Ungasiksikaq* is there and waiting to dance.

The first dancer appears through the curtain, moves in front of the drummers and makes a slight jump toward each side of the room. This is a signal that he wants his own song. If the dancer does not jump, then any song can be sung. A person usually inherits his song from a grandparent. Several brothers often use the same song, or if there is more than one song for their family they may each have a different one. As the dancer's song is begun, his wife comes from behind the curtain too and they dance. At the conclusion of the dance, the couple distributes the gifts amidst laughing and conversation. Those who get presents join the couple in another dance. There is much applause and the couple seat themselves at the side of the dancing area and the next dancer comes in. If a member of *Ungasiksikaq* who has already danced wishes to give a present to a fellow member, he does so when the dancer first enters and before gifts are distributed. Then he joins in the dance with the recipient of the presents.

A woman may sometimes come in first if her husband's song is no longer remembered or if her family's song is customarily used rather than his. Widows may be accompanied by single men and widowers by single women or widows. If a man's wife does not dance he can be accompanied by a son or other relative and the same is true if the man does not dance. Couples who dance also occasionally have a son or daughter dance with them.

The presents that are given at *Kakumisaq* seem to go to relatives, friends, and individuals who are in need. The custom of giving presents is associated with the old autumn ceremonies when a man who had a partner in another ceremonial group sent him a gift, requesting a specified exchange (Rainey, 1947, p. 246). Today the presents are mostly small and inexpensive items such as cigarettes, tubes of beads, gloves, food, and the like, that can be purchased at the store. However, some people give such things as boxes of ammunition, five-gallon cans of kerosene, suitcases, and rifles. Men who have money earned in summer employment often give lavish gifts to relatives and partners.

After all the *Ungasiksikaq* couples have danced, all the members of that ceremonial organization join in a dance and then retire behind the curtain. After a short interval the first dancer comes out and makes a sweeping motion with his arm, telling *Qagmaktoq* to go home and get food to serve to *Ungasiksikaq*. The whole ceremony is then repeated with the roles of the two groups exchanged.

The order in which the ceremonial members perform their dances is not specified except that the first ones to dance are older persons and whaling captains. It is a mark of respect shown to these individuals.

The *kakumisaq* feast-dance was originally associated with the fall ceremonies and followed the series of competitions between the ceremonial organizations. The one that lost the competition fed the winners first. Today, the council has decreed that the *Qagmaktoq* shall always eat first. In the old days the feast would, of course, have taken place in the ceremonial house and the "joy shout" made by the dancers behind the curtain would originally have echoed up through the entrance passage. The curtained-off section of the parish hall is obviously intended to take the place of the entrance passage. I was told that the *kakumisaq* feast-dance died out and was revived only in recent years as part of the Christmas week festivities.

Although Christmas week activities begin in the parish hall in the late afternoon, there are also outdoor events during the mornings. A women's and men's dog race is held and there also are races and other outdoor games for the children if the weather is favorable. In the evenings, prizes are awarded to the winners. As they are presented, other persons may take advantage of the opportunity to give presents to the contestants. A group of singers and guitar players, the "Tigara Playboys," also performs several times during the Christmas week, playing and singing western songs, a type of music particularly liked by the villagers.

Part of one evening during Christmas week is usually devoted to a series of dances which formerly belonged to different ceremonial organizations. Traditionally, these were performed during the autumn ceremonies, but they are now combined and performed at Christmas. One of the dances involves the use of a wooden top *(qepsuk)* around the rim of which a fringe of eagle feathers is fixed in a series of holes. While holding the top, the performer presents four different dances to four different songs, all with one knee on the floor. At the end of the dances, he twirls the top. If many feathers fly there will be good fortune for all; if the top fails to spin or if the feathers do not fly out properly, it is an ill omen. This dance belongs to the *Ungasiksikaq* people and was originally part of an "inviting in" ceremony in which the *Qagmaktoq* people were guests at the *Ungasiksikaq* ceremonial house. A number of these "inviting in" ceremonies were part of the fall cycle of ceremonial activities (Rainey, 1947, pp. 250-51).

Most of today's Christmas dances are connected with *Ungasik-*

sikaq, because a generation ago certain members of that organization were interested in preserving the dances and taught them to
younger people. The dances and songs now performed by a group
of about a dozen persons were formerly enacted by all the members of the ceremonial organization with which a particular song
and dance was associated. The program of dances as seen today
was developed about twenty years ago. However, two or three of
them are remembered as having been performed at Christmas
around 1915.

The last dance formerly held in the ceremonial houses before they
were closed for the winter was the masquerade dance *(wingeruk),*
which was held by both ceremonial groups simultaneously during
one evening. Both men and women went from their own ceremonial
house to the other dressed in outlandish costumes and usually
masked. Each person crawled through the entrance hole of the
ceremonial house and danced alone before his or her *uma,* a person who had the same name as the dancer's wife or husband. Sometimes the dancers rubbed noses with the *uma* (Rainey, 1947, p.
242).

Today, the masquerade dance is always the final event of the
Christmas week festivities and takes place on New Year's Eve.
The dancers enter the parish hall in groups or occasionally one
at a time with stockings or scarves over their faces and with costumes designed to provoke laughs. Men dress like women and vice
versa. As the dancers enter the room, they go to their *umas* and
usually try to kiss them or muss their hair. The *uma* then gives
a little gift such as a pack of cigarettes, chewing gum, or similar article. Mostly young people seem to take part in the masquerade dance today, although everyone enjoys watching the foolery
and horseplay that is associated with it. The dancing continues
until midnight when everyone is in the proper mood of gaiety to
celebrate the arrival of the new year.

Although the remnants of the old Point Hope ceremonial cycle
are confined to the Christmas season, the people are fond of having a variety of entertainment throughout the year, and have developed considerable interest in such outdoor activities as baseball
and old style football, in addition to indoor games, card playing, dances, and moving pictures. The school sponsors parties
of various kinds at Christmas, Halloween, and Valentine's Day,
so that Point Hope children are familiar with a great variety of
American games.

A group of men in the village has organized a baseball club having about thirty members, and charges dues which are used for the

purchase of baseball equipment. The first games of the year are sometimes played as early as the time of the spring whaling feast, after which there is usually a game every Sunday evening, when the weather is favorable, until late in August. When the army had a detachment near Point Hope, the village team had frequent games with them. The villagers also play the crews of visiting Coast Guard boats and other vessels that occasionally anchor in the lee of the Point Hope spit.

The Sunday evening baseball game ends about midnight, after which there are always some who want to play old style football, a game that bears more resemblance to soccer than to American football. The goals are several hundred yards apart; one team tries to kick the ball across the other's goal. Any number of men, women, and children can play this game, but in recent years, the married men play the unmarried men. Formerly, everyone in the village who had a namesake belonged to two sides called *ukormiut* (point or sea people) and *kapkormiut* (land people). The land people kicked toward the west and the sea people toward the east. Since a person belonged to the side of his namesake, households were split up and there was a great deal of joking within households about the game. The game was played during winter evenings, with children usually beginning to play in the late afternoon and adults joining in the evening. According to the old rules, only old men and women were entitled to pick up the ball and throw it (Rainey, 1947, p. 256).

Toward the end of the nineteenth century, when large numbers of coastal and inland Eskimos were camped at Jabbertown during the spring, a great football game was played following the spring whaling feast. The playing field extended as much as ten miles along the spit and the game continued for several days. The visiting Eskimos often far outnumbered the Point Hope people. The visitors always kicked toward the west while Point Hope kicked toward the east. Sometimes there were bitter fights during these games and the great players of that period are still remembered and talked about in the village.

Point Hope people like to play cards and card-playing groups are a significant aspect of visiting patterns in the village. Families characteristically visit one another on Sunday evenings to play cards. A favorite game, particularly among older people, is a form of double solitaire that can be played with two or four persons. The visiting patterns are fairly rigid, the same couples playing with each other time after time. Pinochle is another favor-

ite game. A group of men assembles nearly every night to play
at the store.

Birthday celebrations are enjoyed and there is almost always
some kind of party when a person has a birthday. Birthday parties
for children, such as are familiar in American culture, are unknown. A child's birthday party is for adult friends of the parents
or grandparents, but guests occasionally bring presents for the
child. The entertainment at birthday parties usually consists of
games, or simply conversation. Usually the guests bring food.

On Friday or Saturday night of each week there is generally an
American dance held at the schoolhouse. These are always well
attended and the most active part is taken by people between the
ages of twenty and forty. Practically no one over that age attends.
Music is furnished by a phonograph belonging to the school, the
records being brought by the dancers. The most popular records
are of hillbilly and western music. The dancers are noticeably indifferent to slow pieces and ballads. Various specialty dances such
as the schottische and Virginia reel are popular. The dances often
last until midnight but must end at the discretion of the schoolteacher. The mission holds a dance for young people every Wednesday night after the evening service.

Eskimo dances are held sporadically throughout the year. They
are well attended, but there does not seem to be enough interest
to warrant having more than three or four a year exclusive of
Thanksgiving and Christmas. Some young people appear to be interested in the old dances, but none is skilled in their execution.
Apparently the instances are few where older people teach the
dances to their children or grandchildren.

Perhaps the favorite form of group entertainment is the weekly
motion picture sponsored by the village council. The admission
charge is 25 cents for adults and 15 cents for school children; preschool children are admitted free. The films, which are shown in
the school, seem to appeal to a much wider age group than the
American dances. Even elderly people who do not speak or understand English attend regularly. Attendance varies from seventy-
five to eighty, which is the capacity of the room. The audience is
responsive to situations on the screen and the attention of everyone
is held even when the action can have little or no meaning for some
of the observers. Westerns, with an abundance of action, are the
most readily understood and consequently the most enjoyed. Slap-
stick situations are also meaningful and elicit a prompt response
on the part of all present.

8

THE INDIVIDUAL

AND

THE CULTURE

THE LAWS of Alaska require that every child between the ages of seven and sixteen must attend school unless he has already completed the eighth grade. The Point Hope school is one of the many in Alaska operated by the Bureau of Indian Affairs. It has two teachers, a man and his wife. At various times in the past there has also been a teacher's aid, usually a local person with a high school education, who was in charge of the beginners, or kindergarten group, and the first and second grades. Eight grades are taught in addition to the beginners' class.

The school building, one of the oldest on the Arctic coast, is of frame construction and contains two classrooms and quarters for the teachers. During the summer of 1955, a second school building was constructed, consisting of an additional, more comfortable, and better-lighted schoolroom, and new teachers' quarters. The old building contains a clinic, a school kitchen, and quarters designed for visiting nurses and other Bureau of Indian Affairs personnel.

In addition to their instructional duties, the teachers are expected to concern themselves with the physical well-being of the villagers and to treat minor ailments in the clinic. More serious difficulties, and progress reports on sick individuals, are reported to the doctor in Kotzebue on a nightly radio schedule. The teacher also listens nightly to the Alaska Communications System schedule in order to pick up telegrams for the village. Depending upon the wishes of the schoolteacher, the school building is available for a variety of village functions: weekly movies; the P. T. A. , health council, and village council meetings; and dances.

The Bureau of Indian Affairs nutrition program is carried out at Point Hope in the form of the hot breakfast that is prepared in the school kitchen. The village P. T. A. decided on the hot breakfast as more valuable to the children than a hot lunch. The preparation is done by members of the P. T. A. with two women working each morning. Hot cakes, bacon, eggs, cocoa, hot cereal, vegetables, and the like make up the meal. In addition, milk or fruit juice is served to all the children in the middle of the morning and again in the afternoon.

The law requires a 180-day school year. At Point Hope, most teachers have preferred to carry through from early September until early May with a minimum of vacations. School is usually dismissed during the week that the *North Star* is unloading.

With the exception of the Episcopal priest and his wife, the schoolteachers are the only permanent white residents in the village. Being representatives of the United States government and practically the only contact between the people and the Bureau of Indian Affairs, they have a considerable amount of influence. Formerly, the teachers had even more power because they were also the welfare agents in the various villages, but recently there has been a tendency to give these jobs to other available qualified persons in the villages. However, there is still opportunity for friction between the villagers and the teachers; e. g. , in connection with hauling ice for the school and helping with the nutrition program. Attendance and the removal of children from school for one reason or another also cause difficulty. Teachers have complained bitterly about the consistent tardiness of children whose parents sleep late, and about parents who keep their children home to do chores when there are others in the family who could do them. General reaction to the school is favorable but a few families, not convinced of the value of education, are uncooperative in various ways. The Bureau of Indian Affairs is interested in keeping average daily attendance as high as possible, because the appropriation is in jeopardy if attendance falls off. Every year there is some parental pressure to have older children excused from school to help with whaling. This permission is usually granted, contrary to BIA policy; the parents would probably take their children out of school whether permission were given or not. When the crews are not on the ice, the children attend school as usual.

The school is divided into two sections: one teacher has the beginners and first four grades in one room and the other teacher has grades five through eight in a second room. There were sixty-six children in school during the 1955-56 term, but in the preceding six or eight years there were as many as eighty-eight. Some of the teachers' difficulties are caused by this heavy load and the problems inherent in any system where there is more than one

Plate VII-A. Point Hope School

The school buildings

In school

Plate VII-B. Point Hope School

In school

grade in a single room. Particularly in the lower grades, children become unruly while the teacher is working with another grade.

The Bureau of Indian Affairs curriculum is largely traditional, with emphasis on language, social studies, arithmetic, art, and music, together with whatever variations and additions the teachers desire. At various times, teachers have added shop, homemaking, health, and physical education.

Of necessity, the major instructional emphasis is placed upon oral English and reading; much of the instruction is of a remedial nature. In 1955-56 the children in the first and second grades were unable to read or write at the beginning of the school year; previously there had been a teacher's aid in charge of the beginners and first two grades who, knowing nothing of teaching techniques, merely played games with the children. Many students have advanced to the upper grades without an adequate knowledge of English.

The progress made by the beginners in learning to read and write is directly proportional to the use of English in the home. Children from homes where very little English is spoken are still learning to read, rather than reading to learn.

The attention span in the upper grades is fairly good. Students work quietly. Reading is a slow process. Some of the students, although slow, are very thorough. Written English is most difficult for all the students, even those who can read fairly well, particularly from the standpoint of grammar.

Boys and girls sit apart as much as possible. Desks are divided by grade; the girls all sit on one side or one end. This is less true for the lower grades. There is a great deal of note passing between seventh- and eighth-grade boys and girls, accompanied by much giggling.

Children are almost invariably one to four years older than is normal for their grade because of time lost due to illness or suspected illness. Tuberculosis suspects are sometimes excluded from school and other public gatherings until the results of X-ray or sputum tests are known. These reports are often slow in reaching the village. Of the twenty-five Point Hopers at the high school at Mt. Edgecumbe in 1956, thirteen were over eighteen years of age.

In 1953 the seventh and eighth grades were initiated at Point Hope. Before that time, students had to go to White Mountain for these grades, but very few did so. Before 1953 fewer than twelve Point Hope children reached the Mt. Edgecumbe high school or the industrial school, now closed, located at Eklutna. By 1955-56, however, every Point Hope graduate enrolled at Mt. Edgecumbe. This increase can be credited to the full elementary school program at Point Hope and the present-day interest of the graduates in the world beyond the village.

The high school at Mt. Edgecumbe has an academic course as well as training in various trades. The Mt. Edgecumbe School of Nursing, which is operated in conjunction with the high school, accepts seventeen- to thirty-five-year-old women or men for a one-year course in practical nursing. Graduates are eligible for federal government employment as practical nurses with a civil service rating of GS-3. All the girls that graduated at Point Hope in the spring of 1956 planned to enroll eventually in the nursing school. Some boys expressed interest. The teachers urged all the students to complete the regular high school course first. There are many openings for practical nurses in the larger towns in Alaska, but none at Point Hope or any other native village. It is too early to tell what percentage of Mt. Edgecumbe graduates will return to the village. One man was away from the village for nearly six years, during which time he completed the industrial course at Eklutna. Upon return he found himself unable and unprepared to make a living in the traditional Eskimo manner and had a difficult time until he secured employment in the village store. Two girls who completed high school at Mt. Edgecumbe in 1947 contemplated returning to the village. Their families were not eager to have them at home because they were quite poor at the time. They preferred to have the girls continue their education or get jobs and send money home. Eventually both girls married white men and settled permanently away from the village.[7]

As noted earlier, the population of the entire Arctic coast was depleted by perhaps one half as a result of diseases introduced by the whites. Influenza and tuberculosis are the diseases that have taken the greatest toll of lives at Point Hope, but mumps and whooping cough have also been costly. An examination of several hundred Eskimos in the northwest coastal area by the surgeon of the United States Revenue Steamer *Bear* during the summer of 1890 proved that 85 per cent of those tested were afflicted with some form of syphilis (U. S. Census Bureau, 1893, p. 143). The decline in population in most villages seems to have continued until about the turn of the century, after which the population became stabilized

---

[7]See Hughes, 1960, pp. 312-22, for an analysis of the school's role in another Alaskan Eskimo community.

and is now slowly increasing. The records of St. Thomas' Mission
at Point Hope show a total of 93 births between 1891 and 1900; 123
persons died. From 1931 to 1940 there were 110 births and only 86
deaths. However, in every decade between 1891 and 1940, more
than half the deaths occurred in the under-eighteen-year age group.
Medical care has improved in recent years and the birth rate remains high; therefore a continued population increase may be an-
ticipated, barring other negative factors.

Point Hope mortality figures for the period from January, 1948,
to August, 1956, are shown in the following table as compiled from
St. Thomas' Mission records:

Causes of Death		Deaths by Ages	
Tuberculosis	12	Infants (to one year)	10
Respiratory infections	9	1 to 5 years	9
Unknown	8	6 to 20 years	3
Accident	7	21 to 40 years	8
Heart ailments	3	41 to 65 years	2
Measles	3	66 years and up	19
General decline	3	Total	51
Cancer	2		
Pneumonia	2		
Stillbirth	1		
Blood poisoning	1		
Total	51		

The causes of death are listed by the missionary and do not represent a professional opinion. It is probable that many more deaths
were caused, either directly or indirectly, by tuberculosis, including most of those listed as respiratory ailments. Tuberculosis
has been an important cause of death ever since records were kept.
In 1956 nearly 50 per cent of the population had either active, inactive, or arrested tuberculosis. Syphilis, once a prevalent disease at Point Hope and other Arctic villages, was nearly nonexistent
by 1956, there being but one latent case in the village.

Epidemics still sweep through the village with amazing rapidity
when an infected person comes in from outside. The teacher estimated that 200 persons of the population of 225 were ill during the
influenza and mumps epidemics of April, 1950. In the autumn of
1953, two boys, returning from summer employment, brought
measles to the village. Although they went to bed immediately,
practically the whole village was infected within a few weeks; three
infants died.

The list of deaths by ages shows that infant mortality is still

high, a condition attributable partly to inadequate medical care locally and partly to uncertain transportation to the Public Health
Service hospital at Kotzebue.

The Public Health Service supplies the school clinic with a limited amount of medical equipment that permits the treatment of
minor ailments and also the administering of emergency first aid
to the more serious cases. The teachers, who hold a clinic hour
every evening, maintain a record of those who should receive X
rays upon arrival of the Coast Guard vessel or the *North Star*.
They also know which children must remain away from school because of active tuberculosis and which ones should rest for periods
of time after school.

Parents are quick to consult the teacher if a child is ill but the
will of the child often influences the decision of the parent to administer medication that the teacher recommends. All parents are
prompt in seeing that their children keep appointments with the
visiting public health nurse. Today there seem to be few theories,
religious, magical, or otherwise, to account for disease; it is
something that is simply accepted. However, some people have
their own ideas about what is wrong and do not put much faith in
what the teacher or visiting nurse tells them. However, only in
cases where understanding between the teacher or visiting nurse
and the villagers breaks down are people reluctant to accept medical advice.

In the course of a year, the teacher may administer as many as
800 treatments in the school clinic but these, of course, outnumber
those administered in the home. The school records suggest that
most teachers are reluctant to go into the homes of the seriously
ill. The Point Hopers consider medical aid to be an important part
of the teacher's duties and are inclined to judge, not on ability to
teach, but rather on willingness to "help the people." A teacher who
makes frequent calls to the homes of sick people, or makes sure
that children who are confined to their homes by illness receive
hot lunches, is admired and respected.

The teachers, and occasional visiting nurses, are aided in their
medical work in the village by the Women's Health Council. This
group consists of ten women whose duties include checking on
people who are sick, distributing medicine from the school clinic,
assisting with the tuberculosis chemotherapy program, weighing
school children, and acting as assistants to public health teams
that come to the village. At one time members of the health council
made regular inspections of all houses in the village to see that
they were kept clean. However, this was resented by householders

and consequently dropped. The village council and other organizations are cooperative when problems concerning health arise. During my stay, the village council and the Mothers' Club contributed funds for the purchase of vitamin pills for the preschool children, and the village has also purchased supplies of penicillin.

Villagers undergo periodic tests for tuberculosis. A United States Coast Guard vessel makes yearly stops at the village to take X rays and perform other medical services. An attempt is made to get the people with active tuberculosis into sanitariums in southeastern Alaska, but in 1956 there was usually much delay, sometimes due to lack of beds or transportation but sometimes because of administrative difficulties. In the past some men have refused to go to the hospital because of worry over provision for their families. Today it is possible for a woman whose husband is in the sanitarium to obtain Aid to Dependent Children, one of the social security programs.

When tuberculosis patients return from the hospital, they encounter problems in carrying out the medically prescribed program of home treatment that stresses the need for regular living habits. Regularity is not a characteristic of village households nor is it possible in homes where large numbers of people live in a single room. Most families, however, make an effort to maintain the regular schedules recommended.

A public health nurse stationed in Kotzebue makes periodic visits to the village, mostly for the purpose of administering vaccinations. Most people of all ages have received shots for typhoid fever, smallpox, whooping cough, tetanus, and diphtheria. While I was in the village, Salk vaccine was given to all children up to nineteen years of age. The nurse usually stays for a week or more, once a year, to give typhoid booster shots, examine the teeth and tonsils of children, hold a baby clinic, and examine pregnant women. During the summer of 1956, she held a series of first-aid classes and discussed various health problems with the health council. The doctor stationed at Kotzebue Hospital does not visit the villages except in cases of extreme emergency. Occasionally doctors on research projects pay brief visits to the village, but they seldom have the time or the inclination to perform routine medical services.

The chemotherapy program for arresting tuberculosis by treatment in the home is a responsibility of the public health nurse. Two members of the health council act as chemotherapy aides. A clinic is held once a week by the aides who check on bed rest and weight, give medicine, and otherwise carry out the instructions of the nurse. In August, 1956, there were nineteen individuals, mostly children, on chemotherapy.

In 1956 the Territorial Department of Health instituted a sanitation program, largely educational, in many Alaskan villages. A sanitation aide was chosen from the village and sent to Fairbanks for a month of training; supervision is provided by a district sanitarian. The program is intended to improve sanitary conditions in the village, particularly with regard to drinking water and waste disposal. Sanitation is not so much of a problem at Point Hope as it is in many Alaskan villages, because of the location of the village on a clean, well-drained gravel beach.

Point Hope is becoming increasingly health conscious; I noted numerous homes in which attempts were made to carry out health suggestions made by the health council and visiting nurses. Drinking water is not boiled but some mothers boil the water that they use in formulas for their babies. Since most of the drinking water used during the winter months comes from melted snow gathered in the village, more extensive boiling of drinking water would be a protection against diarrhea and other intestinal disorders that are quite prevalent in the village.

In spite of the fact that mothers bathe their small children frequently, impetigo is common among preschool and school children. In winter, moisture condensing on a parka ruff often causes a rash on the face, a condition favorable to impetigo. Children get quite dirty in their outdoor play; when families are large, mothers have to rely upon older children to keep themselves clean.

Older children and adults relieve themselves outside during the summer when the weather is good. At other times, a bucket or large can is used and emptied some distance from the house when full. Some families keep their slop bucket in the storm shed except in very cold weather but apparently there is no use of toilet chemicals. One girl, recently returned from Mt. Edgecumbe, was successful in persuading her family to build a partitioned "bathroom" in the house. People who live in the edge of town are less particular where they dump their waste than those living in the center. They are able to dump their waste on the beach where few people will encounter it.

Home remedies are extensively used, and a number of individuals have acquired reputations as amateur medical experts. One woman is always called upon to examine and massage twisted ankles, sprained wrists, or muscular injuries of any kind. A particular man is considered an expert at pulling teeth with dental forceps borrowed from the clinic. Cures for diarrhea include the eating of quantities of flour that has been browned in a frying pan, and drinking a very strongly brewed tea, even eating the leaves. Many people believe that a piece of blubber rubbed on a cut of any kind will speed the healing although they admit that the nurse would not favor this remedy. Other home remedies are extensively used but almost never to the exclusion of advice from the school clinic.

The Social Security Act, passed by Congress in 1935, became effective in Alaska in 1937 and provides, on the Old-Age Assistance Program, for a monthly assistance to those over sixty-five years of age. The law has been in effect for twenty years, but only in the last ten have Department of Public Welfare representatives been appointed in the remote villages, and the people made aware of their eligibility. The first social security was in the form of old-age benefits. In 1945, Aid to Dependent Children was added, and in 1951, Aid to the Blind. It is the duty of the welfare representative to accept and forward applications for the various types of assistance. Representatives receive $2.00 for each new welfare case handled. In many villages the schoolteacher is the welfare agent, but the Department of Public Welfare tries to appoint a local person if there is one who can handle the paper work. At Point Hope the postmaster has the job. He is generally considered to be fair and there are few complaints.

In 1956 thirteen individuals received Old-Age Assistance for a total of $880 per month or slightly more than $67.00 per month per person. Five families received Aid to Dependent Children at a total of $432 per month. A monthly payment is fixed for each child; to be eligible the head of the family must be incapacitated for work. This form of assistance is particularly significant for widows and families where the father is in a sanitarium. Unwed mothers are also eligible if the father cannot be determined and if there are no other male members of the family who can assist in the support of the child. In 1956, there were no persons in the village receiving Aid to the Blind.

The Bureau of Indian Affairs formerly had a program that allowed destitute individuals to obtain supplies of various kinds from the village store and repay by doing work for the school. Payment could also be taken from old-age or other assistance checks. Assistance was also given to sick people and others who were in need but had no prospects of being able to make a repayment. The family of a person who died destitute could obtain money for funeral expenses from the Bureau of Indian Affairs. This program was discontinued about 1952.

In families where there is an old person a large number of people often are indirectly dependent upon the monthly old-age assistance check. This income has greatly strengthened the position of old people, who formerly were dependent entirely on their relatives for support. Old people without families were often destitute in earlier days and sometimes were forced to beg from neighbors. Similarly, the position of widows has been greatly improved by the payment of Aid to Dependent Children. Formerly widows were entirely dependent upon the charity of their relatives and usually returned to their parents' homes after their husbands died. They now are able to set up and maintain independent homes.

In 1880 Captain C. L. Hooper in command of the U. S. Revenue Steamer *Corwin* cruising in the Arctic Ocean, commented that "I believe that every man, woman, and child in Arctic Alaska smokes a pipe." (Hooper, 1881, p. 60.) Fifty years ago all the whaling vessels stocked tobacco for trade purposes and several early explorers in the area reported that the Eskimos had a great desire for it. Today at Point Hope, a large number of adults smoke, particularly women. Smoking is not confined to any particular group, but is found among those over fifteen years of age. A surprisingly large number of older women smoke heavily. Most popular are cigarettes, among young and old. Young men and women apparently smoke nothing else. A few middle-aged and older men smoke pipes, as does one old woman. Plug chewing-tobacco and snuff are used by a few of the oldest men.

Smoking seems to be practiced by a number of school-age boys without, or in spite of, parental objection, but the teachers do not allow smoking in the school building at any time, by school-age boys and girls, even at village functions not connected with the school. Smaller children are aware of the fact that smoking is considered "not good" for children.

It has previously been mentioned that during the latter half of the nineteenth century, when whaling vessels frequented the Arctic Ocean, the Eskimos at Point Hope and other coastal villages received supplies of whisky in exchange for baleen, and also learned to make their own intoxicating liquors from flour and molasses. Although the importation of liquor in very large amounts ceased with the end of commercial whaling, the people continued to make "home brew" according to methods taught them by the whalers.

Today the village of Point Hope, like many in Alaska, is "dry" by local option, meaning that no intoxicating beverages can be sold in the village, or brought in from outside for the purpose of sale. However, there is nothing to prohibit an individual from ordering liquor for his own consumption. The village council imposes a heavy fine on anyone caught making "home brew," and partly because of this rule, and the fact that commercially made liquor tastes much better, local stills have largely disappeared.

The liquor that comes into the village at the present time is ordered by individuals from liquor stores in Nome and Fairbanks. The purchasers, mostly young men, are fairly numerous but few, if any, have enough money to order regularly. Several who were receiving unemployment compensation placed regular orders as did men who had recently returned from summer employment away from the village. I observed no open drinking during my stay at the village. A person receiving a liquor order would pick it up at the plane and take it directly to his home. Occasionally a few young men would get together, usually at the home of a young married couple, and have a drinking party. Nearly all those who order liquor drink until they become drunk, but nearly always manage to do so without creating a public disturbance. Occasionally someone appears slightly intoxicated at a village dance, much to the amusement of all present, but no action is taken unless a complaint is brought before the village council. Several of my friends who received occasional liquor shipments drank in moderation and managed to make a small supply last a long time. However, these individuals were exceptional in this respect.

Most Point Hopers, including some who never order liquor when at home, drink heavily when away from the village. A few young men spend most of their summer's wages on liquor in Fairbanks. The Alaska National Guard encampment at Anchorage is also an opportunity for heavy drinking.

The attitudes toward drinking in the village itself seem to be sharply divided. Older people object and feel strongly that it should not be permitted, while younger persons and many of the middle-aged have no strong feelings against it and will always drink if they get the chance. Nearly everyone feels that drinking is "bad" and some old people are very active, at least verbally, in their condemnation of those who drink. The mission's opposition carries considerable weight with certain elements of the population. People in general, and women in particular, are afraid of those who are drunk, even though such persons are generally peaceful. Occasionally fights break out and family disputes involving personal antagonisms often come to the surface under the influence of liquor.

As in many other small towns, gossip is a potent force in Point Hope and the impartial listener can hear something unfavorable about practically every person in the village. People are distrustful toward their neighbors, mostly, it seems, without cause. Although derogatory comments about other people are common in conversation, I observed no cases in which such feelings broke out into overt conflict. Stories of fights and tongue lashings were related to me, but in general the people go to great lengths to prevent outbreaks of any kind. People who repeat malicious information about each other will behave as friends when they meet in the store or in each other's homes. Because the village is small, and so many of the subsistence activities are cooperative in nature, the Point Hopers fully realize the necessity of getting along together and preserving the social equilibrium at all costs. Many people complain about the amount of gossip and everyone dislikes a "busybody." Individuals whose behavior has been a source of gossip complain long and loudly about village attitudes, but are the first themselves to pass on a derogatory bit of information about someone else.

Village opinion also condemns those who are "bossy" and who tell lies. Individuals usually do not give orders to others, at least outside the family, and resent such behavior. Even whaling captains are unpopular if they give too many orders to their crew members. Chronic lying was practically nonexistent as far as my observations were concerned, but several individuals had reputations as liars, and people were not only disdainful of them, but joked about them.

Family feuds, formerly a vital factor in community life and a great source of danger to those involved, seem to be practically nonexistent. However, power struggles between families for a controlling voice in village political and economic affairs have occurred in recent years and at the present time minor feuds exist. These seem to be based mostly on interpersonal antagonism and do not extend to all members of both families.

The general Point Hope reaction to white people is one of curiosity and overt friendliness. The villagers are anxious to know white people and are markedly uncritical in their approach to them. The categories of whites most familiar are schoolteachers and missionaries, soldiers and construction workers. It was my experience that most of the villagers were unable to see the defects or even the differences in the character of white men. This lack of critical approach is doubtless the result of limited contact with whites, inasmuch as an entirely different set of criteria seems to be adopted when dealing with members of their own race. Also, most village dealings with whites are for a relatively short time and there is limited opportunity for critical evaluation of character.

As the villagers become increasingly aware of developments in the outside world, the more perceptive ones note that the problems of the world are building up and passing on without reference to the Eskimo; the Eskimo has no part to play in them and the problems of the outside world affect him in only the most marginal way. The world view of the villagers has been changed greatly as a result of the acculturation process, and those who tend to think about it realize what a small part they play in the over-all picture. They wonder why it is that Eskimos are on the outside of things today. White men are vitally interested in the Eskimo area, but their interest and their work has little or no reference to Eskimo culture. It should be reiterated that only the most perceptive individuals are apt to have this point of view and even among them there is very little verbalizing on the subject. However, the feeling of not belonging is often evident in daily contacts, without the necessity of direct conversational reference.

9

VILLAGE ECONOMICS

AS EARLY as 1912, trading vessels were making frequent stops at Point Hope during the summer months and leaving stocks of goods to be traded to the local people for furs and baleen. However, it was not until 1920 that a store, owned and operated by villagers, came into existence. In that year the mission sent out an order for merchandise with money collected from thirteen individuals. The store was virtually run by the mission and the shareholders met each year to choose a storekeeper. The individual who owned the most stock was elected storekeeper and held the job for several years. At first the store was located at Jabbertown and did strictly a cash business; no furs or native products were handled. The inventory was extremely limited, consisting mostly of clothing and a little food.

In 1926 the store was reorganized and became the Point Hope Trading Company. All connection with the mission was dropped. At first, the reindeer operations were combined with the store and the organization was known as the Point Hope Reindeer and Trading Company, with a board of directors elected from the shareholders. Two members of the board were elected each year for a four-year term and a new president was elected every year. Generally those persons owning the largest amounts of stock were elected to the board. In the late 1920's the store separated from the reindeer company, probably because the former was much more successful.

In 1940 there were approximately forty shareholders. When business was going well, the store paid 10 per cent annual return on money invested. At that time the company was doing about $5,000 worth of business annually. A storekeeper received $50.00 a month in trade or cash, living quarters, and fuel. An assistant storekeeper received $15.00 a month in cash or trade and six sacks of coal per month. During the early years of the store's independent existence there was very little cash in the village, and furs, skins, and products of local manufacture were taken in exchange for food and other merchandise. The fact that fur prices were high at that time greatly influenced the success of the store. Arrangements were made with a trading vessel to take the furs to Seattle during the early summer and return in the autumn with goods for the store.

In 1945, unfavorable conditions developed. Four of the directors of the Point Hope Trading Company were from one extended family and were said to run the village. People requesting certain items were told that they were not for sale. They were, in fact, reserved for the directors and certain other privileged shareholders. The ill feeling reached a climax when the store manager (also a director) retired after eighteen years of service and was presented a gift of $2,000 by the directors without the consent of the other shareholders. Feeling came to be that the store was of little or no service to those who were not shareholders or to many of those who were.

In the spring of 1946, the village took over the store and paid the shareholders $22,700 borrowed from a revolving credit fund available to Indian chartered corporations such as Point Hope. The total amount borrowed was $35,000, part of which was used to purchase merchandise, gasoline boats, and lighterage equipment belonging to the trading company. A list of shareholders was drawn up and the sum due them was divided on a prorated basis in proportion to the individual shareholder's ownership in the company.

The store then became affiliated with the Alaska Native Industries Cooperative Association,[8] a nonprofit cooperative purchasing agency operated through the Department of the Interior. The debt of $35,000 to the United States was to be repaid according to a schedule that has been modified several times and, in 1956, was being repaid at the rate of $3,500 a year. This schedule was maintained and the debt paid on August 1, 1960, at which time ownership of the store was transferred to the village. At the time of liquidation of the Point Hope Trading Company, the village council agreed that future net profits made by the store would remain deposited in the store's account with the Alaska Native Industries Cooperative Association and would under no circumstance be distributed as cash dividends. In this way, it would serve as a reserve to care for all emergen-

---

[8]Characteristically referred to as ANICA, an abbreviation which will be used in the following pages.

cies and to increase the purchasing power of the store. Now that the store is a village-owned cooperative it is hoped that the profits can be used to institute civic improvements that will benefit the village as a whole.

The present-day Point Hope Native Store is a recently constructed frame building with corrugated metal exterior. It consists of a single large room where the selling of merchandise is carried on, a smaller room directly behind this which is used for warm storage and the manager's office, and an unheated storage room behind that. The manager's residence is attached to this building and three unattached warehouses make up the set of store buildings. The merchandise is stocked on shelves on either side of the main room, with dry goods on one side and groceries and hardware on the other. There is also a bulletin board near the door where notices concerning village events are posted. Most of the selling is done by the assistant store manager, while the manager keeps books and writes letters; there is considerable paper work associated with the job. The store has an electric plant that furnishes light to the store and residence. Oil space-heaters are operated continuously during the winter months to keep the merchandise from freezing. In 1956, the store manager was paid $165 a month and received his house and heat free. The assistant store manager received $100 a month flat rate. Both store officials are considerably underpaid in terms of the work that they do but the village council never raises the pay except under strong pressure from those holding the jobs.

Today the store does a strictly cash business except for the handling of furs and products of local manufacture in exchange for merchandise. The annual inventory totals more than $30,000. This figure represents the cost of the merchandise at Seattle plus the agent's service charge (ANICA is the buyer), the freight charge from Seattle to Point Hope, and marine insurance. It is general policy of the store to mark up Seattle prices approximately 50 per cent on all items sold. The markup is on wholesale, not retail, prices. In preparing his merchandise order for the ensuing year, the store manager does not order haphazardly or capriciously, but according to demand. Over the years, it has become clear what food articles sell the best and they are invariably included in the order. The manager posts a notice some time before the order must be sent so that people may order specific things that they want.

In 1956 there was more money in the village than ever before, resulting in a profitable business for the store. In January of 1947,

shortly after the village took over the store, it was doing approximately $3,000 worth of business each year. The following figures,
showing the monthly statements of store operations from September, 1955, to May, 1956, indicate the increase in sales over the
past few years.

	September 1955	October 1955	November 1955	December 1955
(1)	$ 234.28	$ 252.44	$ 186.45	$ 604.22
(2)	5,540.50	7,640.16	6,263.57	5,974.68
(3)	92.91	34.75	41.75	105.55
(4)	5,867.69	7,927.35	6,491.77	6,684.45

	January 1956	February 1956	March 1956	April 1956	May 1956
(1)	$ 860.80	$1,201.62	$1,433.04	$ 928.61	$ 899.48
(2)	4,168.90	4,039.18	4,927.11	4,531.55	5,416.82
(3)	71.35	592.79	280.94	1,086.80	1,329.03
(4)	5,101.05	5,833.59	6,641.09	6,546.96	7,645.33

Key: (1) Goods exchanged for furs or marketable native products
      (2) Goods sold for cash
      (3) Furs and native products sold locally
      (4) Total sales

As already noted, the purchasing power of the village has been
greatly increased in recent years due to the increased summer
employment.

In spite of this gain in business, the store is permitted to increase its yearly order of merchandise only a small amount depending upon the size of its deposit in the Seattle bank and always,
of course, allowing for the payment due according to the loan agreement. Thus, if the store manager wishes to increase his order of
groceries, he must do so largely at the expense of hardware, dry
goods, or fuel oil. The store does not adequately fill the needs of
the villagers, because of this inability to keep up with village purchasing power, and probably will not do so until the loan is fully
repaid. [As of 1961, the loan had been repaid, and the situation
may have changed.]

The store does a large business in furs, skins, and products
of local manufacture. Whalebone masks, ivory carvings, and baleen baskets are bought on consignment from the villagers and
shipped to the Alaska Native Arts and Crafts Association in Juneau,
which disposes of them to retail merchants. The individual craftsman receives two thirds of the selling price at once and the other

third, minus a 2 per cent handling charge, when the item is sold. No money changes hands in these transactions; the sellers receive a credit at the store. In the summer, many old people dig in the Old Tigara site west of the village for artifacts which they hope to dispose of at the store. Since relatively few tourists pass through Point Hope, there is not a large sale for artifacts. Occasionally ANAC takes shipments, but will purchase only items in good condition.

Raw sealskins, including bearded seal, are purchased and disposed of through ANICA or to traders in other Alaskan villages. The price paid for sealskins depends partly upon quotations from Seattle fur buyers. During the winter of 1956, small skins brought $1.25 each and large ones $1.50, the full amount being paid to the seller at the time of the sale. Occasionally, a particularly large or fine skin will bring more. Bearded-seal skins are not normally sold because they are needed locally for boot soles and boat covers. During 1955 the store purchased 3,000 sealskins and was successful in finding a market for all of them. In the spring and winter the people have very little source of money except sealskins, and it is at that time that most of the skins are taken to the store. Quite a number of whole seals are purchased during the winter months when seal hunting is good. They are sold locally in the early spring when people are busy with whaling and are low on dog food. A small seal sells for about $4.00 and a large one for $5.00. Of this amount, at least $1.25 is returnable when the skin is sold at the store. With the exception of polar-bear skins, the store does not do a large business in furs. Fox prices are comparatively low. Large skins in excellent condition seldom bring more than $15.00 or $20.00. Wolverines are occasionally sold to the store, but are more generally used locally for parka ruffs. Furs, like locally manufactured products, are purchased on consignment, two thirds of the price being paid in store credit to the seller at the time of sale.

The purchase and sale of polar-bear skins is by far the largest part of the store's fur business. Polar bears are plentiful in the Point Hope area and between thirty-five and seventy-five animals are killed each winter. In 1956, the store paid $10.00 per foot for polar-bear skins and for several years has been able to sell them all to a single buyer in Seattle. The hunter receives half the price as soon as the skin is prepared and stretched, the rest being paid when the skin is sold. The skin of an adult bear averages from eight to ten feet in length and the best hunters get two or three during a single winter.

In the past ANICA has encouraged villages with stores under its

jurisdiction to develop trade in local products. At Point Hope, a
great deal of interest was shown in the possibility of marketing
seal and whale oil, and as late as 1950 the store shipped forty
drums to Seattle on the *North Star*, mostly to be used in the manufacture of candles and soap. However, this project proved un-
profitable and was dropped. A similar situation developed with
regard to coal, a rather poor grade of which is obtainable by surface mining methods in the Cape Lisburne region. The ANICA offered to buy coal from Point Hope to sell to other villages if it
could be obtained for less than they were paying in Seattle. At the
time this project was under consideration in the early 1940's, local men could be hired to mine and transport the coal for as little
as $1.00 a day plus food; but with increased employment possibili-
ties and rising wages, the mining of coal became impractical and
a satisfactory arrangement with ANICA was never reached. By
1956, no one went to the mines, even to obtain coal for personal
use, because of the time involved, the uncertainty of the weather,
and the possibility of putting the summer months to more profitable use.[9]

A few weeks before I left the village, another store was opened
by a Point Hope man who ordered merchandise by air. He ordered
items that were sold out at the village store and seemed to have
no trouble disposing of them, although his prices were high. He
placed a large order to be delivered on the *North Star* which, although operated by the Bureau of Indian Affairs, carries commercial freight also. The new storekeeper is a local man, but he is
backed principally by an organization directed by former ANICA
employees for the express purpose of competing with ANICA. It
remains to be seen whether this new commercial venture will be
successful, but it is probable that the villagers will gladly transfer
their business if the prices are lower.[10] People have always complained of the high prices in the village store and do not seem to
have much loyalty to it.

Although much of the villager's money income is spent locally,
there is also considerable mail-order business. In recent years
people have become aware of the advantages of mail-order buying,

---

[9]An excellent detailed discussion of the history, development,
and operation of a similar store in another Alaskan Eskimo community will be found in Hughes, 1960, pp. 169-87.

[10]During the winter of 1959, this store burned and in 1960 had
not yet reopened.

and catalogues of all varieties now arrive in great numbers. In addition to the large mail-order houses, several small army-surplus outfits send catalogues and many people order army-surplus equipment, particularly winter clothing, from them.

All Point Hopers operate within two separate and simultaneous economic systems, a money economy and a subsistence economy. Wants developed through contacts with American culture require money for their satisfaction. At the same time, most needs are satisfied by subsistence activities and by far the greatest amount of time is spent in carrying out these activities. Although some families live close to the subsistence level, the goal of all families is to achieve a situation where a money income supplements a livelihood based upon subsistence activities.

As was mentioned previously, money income was a negligible feature of village life until about 1950. Even in the days when fur prices were high, it is doubtful whether much cash was brought into the village, the bulk of the trappers' income being tied up as credit at the store. In 1939, the teacher estimated the average family income as $50.00 per family. In 1948, half the families in the village had an income between $500 and $800 per year, while in 1955, the distribution of estimated income by families was recorded as follows:

Under $100	$100-$199	$200-$299	$300-$399	$400-$499
2	1	2	1	3

$500-$749	$750-$999	$1,000-$1,499	$1,500-$1,999
9	7	15	10

These figures were obtained from records compiled by the Bureau of Indian Affairs and are supposed to include both earned income and an estimated cash value for native products. Since it is practically impossible to estimate the money value of things such as seals, tomcod, and whale meat, the foregoing figures should be considered as only approximate. It appears, though, that half the families in the village have an income of more than $1,000 a year, most of which doubtless comes from summer employment.

Figures are also available on total wages earned by villagers during a year, but again there is some doubt as to whether the estimates are accurate. According to these figures the total wages earned in 1946 by Point Hopers, which would include those employed in the village at year-round jobs, was $3,545. In 1955 the figure was $53,841. These figures at least show the remarkable increase in the purchasing power of the village which has, generally speaking, been converted to a more comfortable standard of living.

One result of increased summer employment has been unemployment compensation, which is now an important source of income in the village. In 1956 anyone who earned more than $500 in a year, and had been laid off from his job, was eligible to receive unemployment compensation providing not more than three quarters of his income had been earned in one quarter of the year. This ruling was meant to eliminate seasonal workers, but most Point Hope men, particularly those employed on construction jobs, work during at least two quarters of the year. Other forms of income mentioned earlier that are of some importance are Old-Age Assistance, Aid to Dependent Children, and, to a lesser degree, National Guard salaries.

Since a certain amount of cash is absolutely essential for such things as fuel for lamps, ammunition, and staple food products like flour, coffee, sugar, and tea, individuals occasionally have need to borrow money for essentials; two village organizations grant small loans. The Mothers' Club, with a treasury of approximately $55.00, grants small loans without interest, mostly to old people who are expecting welfare checks that have been delayed. The village council also allows money to be borrowed from village funds at 2 per cent interest monthly. When the amount set aside for loans has been exhausted, no one can borrow until others have repaid their loans. A number of people borrow from the missionary and occasionally from the schoolteacher, but there seems to be very little borrowing and lending of money between villagers.

There are some families that do not share in the comparative economic prosperity of recent years and have difficulty in maintaining themselves even at the lowest subsistence level. When hunting is poor and there are food and fuel shortages in the village, it is usually the same families that are the most acute sufferers. These are the poor hunters, men who work hard enough but just do not seem to be able to make a go of it. There are lazy individuals too; men who do not go hunting regularly and make no attempt to obtain summer employment. In most cases, the unsuccessful men are heads of large families and have difficulty in clothing and feeding them. The problems faced by some of these families will be more fully discussed in the case studies.

Ownership of capital goods plays an important part in the ability of a man to provide for his family and to take full advantage of the subsistence activities that are open to him. If a man has a good rifle, dogs, a skin boat, and the like, he is in much better position to be a successful provider. It is no coincidence that the men in the village who are considered to be the best hunters are those with good equipment in good condition. A man who has poor equipment for hunting has a difficult time improving his lot because he is never successful enough as a hunter to get ahead of the cause of his difficulty. A man without dogs will find it impossible to get to the open water, when it is far from the village, in time to shoot enough seals so that he can support dogs. His wife will be unable to go up the Kukpuk River for fall fishing. Summer employment has done much to enable many families to improve their lot and to rise above the level of bare subsistence.

The following brief case studies of individual families are intended to show the range of living standards within the village and the reasons why some families enjoy a higher standard of living than others.

Family A consists of a man, his wife, four children, and his mother-in-law, who are living in a house owned by the mother-in-law. The man is an excellent and indefatigable hunter whose success is partly due to the fact that he has the use of equipment that belonged to his deceased father-in-law. He is also the captain of a whaling crew that was formerly headed by his father-in-law. During the summer he works in Kotzebue or Fairbanks and has worked at Cape Lisburne. A member of a building trades union, he has considerable skill as a carpenter and is also qualified to do electrical work and plumbing. During his most successful summers, he has earned as much as $2,000. The family likes American foods and clothing and will buy them whenever money is available. As a result, they are usually well dressed and well fed. Because the head of the family has good dogs and good equipment, there is always enough to eat even when money is scarce. In addition, the aged mother-in-law receives an old-age assistance check every month. The family spends much of its cash income on luxury items, food and clothing, a radio, outboard motor, and sewing machine. Family A is a good example of a modern Eskimo family that is successful in utilizing all aspects of a rapidly changing cultural environment.

Family B, consisting of a man about forty, his wife, and six children, is one of the most unsuccessful families in the village for a variety of reasons. The family head is in poor health and a mediocre hunter. As a result there is seldom enough to eat in the house and the children are often poorly clothed. The man, who speaks good English, occasionally goes to Fairbanks in the summer to work for a mining company, but invariably spends all his money and returns to the village with nothing. The family has been on relief many times in the past and lives at the bare subsistence level. The house contains no luxuries whatever and is poorly maintained. The wife is sloppy and does not encourage her husband to be a better provider. This is a poorly adapted Eskimo family from an economic standpoint but they are nevertheless fully integrated socially into community life.

Family C, consisting of a man, aged thirty-six, his wife, and four children, is unique in the village in that they live almost entirely on the income from a full-time job held by the man at the school. This family head is better educated than anyone else in the village and is well equipped to handle a job that often calls for making contacts with outsiders. His ability in this regard is recognized by the community which has elected him president of the village council. This family enjoys the highest level of living in the village and always has plenty to eat, good clothes, and luxuries, and is saving money for the purchase of a larger house. Because of his full-time job, the family head can hunt only on week ends, but is fairly successful as a hunter nevertheless, and of course is in a position to buy meat from other hunters. The family purchases heavily at the store and through the mail. Other families would like to live as this family does, enjoying the advantages of steady year-round employment and yet having some time to pursue the local subsistence activities.

Family D is another family with a low standard of living, mostly due to the fact that the family head is a poor hunter and consequently has no incentive for a vigorous approach to subsistence activities. He has no dogs and very little equipment of any kind. Although he speaks good English, because of army experience, he does not belong to a union and therefore is unable to obtain profitable summer employment. In the past, he, his wife, and three children have had relief allotments during the winter months. Some of his wife's relatives are angry because of the low standard of living his wife and children are forced to endure.

Family E's head is responsible for the support of his wife, five children, two grandchildren, and a variety of affinal relatives. Fortunately, he is one of the best hunters in the village, being nearly always successful even when others fail. He has good hunting equipment, but the weight of his economic responsibilities keeps the family's standard of living from ever rising far above the bare subsistence level. A member of the carpenter's union, this family head has the most successful summer employment record in the village, but his earnings are barely sufficient to supplement local foods for the large number of dependents. Although he is much sought after as a whaling crew member, it is indicative of this man's struggle to provide food for his large family that he has never been able to save enough to become a captain himself.

Family F, consisting of a forty-year-old man, his wife, and five children, is a striking example of a family not well adapted to arctic living because of the inefficiency of the family head. He works as hard as other men but usually has very little to show for his efforts. He speaks practically no English and therefore does not work outside the village. What little money the family earns comes from housework that his wife does for the schoolteachers. In spite of the struggles to maintain themselves the children are always adequately clothed, although not always adequately fed. This is a family that had not been successful in meeting the requirements of both a money and a subsistence economy.

Family G, in contrast to Family D, represents an almost perfect combination of the two economies. The family head, a man of forty, who supports his wife and three children, is fully aware of all employment opportunities and never fails to take full advantage of his union membership. He is always in contact with his union, keeps his dues paid, and finds jobs that pay well. He invests most of his summer savings in capital equipment that increases his chances of being a successful hunter. His dog team is generally considered to be the best in the village and he has recently become a whaling captain. This man represents the most successful type of younger Eskimo, who is able to achieve success both in his own and an alien culture. It is these men who can take full advantage of the economic possibilities of both cultures that are the successful modern Eskimos of today.

Family H comes as close as any to living on a strictly subsistence basis and almost entirely on local foods. The family head, who supports a wife and five children, is an excellent hunter who works harder at hunting than anyone in the village. Their home contains no luxuries and the only items they purchase from the store are coffee, tea, sugar, milk, flour, nonleaded gas, and ammunition. When money is needed this family head makes masks and jewelry that he can sell to the store for credit. Since he is a good hunter, seal, polar-bear, and fox skins also provide him with store credit. The family is traditionally oriented from an economic standpoint, but is moderately successful and free from want because of the family head's skill as a hunter.

Family I is an example of a family that lives mostly on Old-Age Assistance received by the man and by his wife. The couple have a

twenty-five-year-old unmarried son who hunts some and provides
the family with a certain amount of local foods. A married daughter, her husband, and two children are also parts of the family.
The son-in-law is an expert ivory carver and brings some money
to the family in that way. This family relies heavily on purchases
from the store and is often badly in need of money at the end of
the month just before checks arrive. Welfare checks would be
adequate for the support of the individuals for whom they are intended, but often others are dependent upon them as well. In some
cases this is a reasonable arrangement, since old people can thus
repay assistance from younger relatives in carrying out daily activities.

10

RELIGION

The Role of the Church in Village Life

St. Thomas' Mission of the Episcopal Church, established at
Point Hope in 1890, is in the charge of a resident priest, assisted
by a villager who acts as interpreter at the services and is a part-
time maintenance employee of the mission. The Church is represented in the village by the church council, an organization that
more or less corresponds to the vestry of a regular Episcopal
parish church. The council at Point Hope was originally appointed
by the Bishop of Alaska, but now its representatives are selected
by the priest. The interpreter acts as president of the church council.

The main duties of the church council are to help the priest
run the mission. Each member is licensed by the bishop as a lay
reader and, theoretically, at least, each one is capable of carrying out all the services of the Church except sacraments. Council
members are proud of their positions as lay readers; in their
homes, one often finds the license framed and hanging on the wall.
One member of the council conducts the Sunday evening services
each week while another builds a fire in the church every Sunday
so that it will be warm by the time the morning services begin.
When the priest is away, they operate the mission and conduct
services. The council also conducts all services and other affairs
of the mission when there is no priest in residence, as has been
the case occasionally.

In addition to the services, the mission sponsors a number of
community activities. The Girl Scouts, affiliated with the group
in Fairbanks, are directed by the missionary's wife. The girls
sew, do other kinds of needlework, cook, read the scout hand-
book, and perform other appropriate scout activities. The acolytes,

151

a regular Episcopal Church group, are a group of boys who assist the priest during the church services. Every boy who has been confirmed and is still in school is an acolyte. The group meets with the priest on Saturday afternoons to play games, clean the church, and do other church activities. The Altar Guild, another regular Episcopal Church organization which is active at the mission, consists of a group of women who take care of the altar equipment (linen, candlesticks, communion services, and so on). There is also a loosely organized Women's Club that is in charge of the sale of old clothes that are sent to the mission.

There are three church services every week in the village. On Sunday morning there is the regular service of Morning Prayer and sermon with a celebration of the Holy Communion on alternate weeks. Sermons are preached in English but are translated for the congregation. A Sunday evening service is also held, as well as Evening Prayer on Wednesday followed by games and a dance for the young people. Both these services are held in the parish hall.

Children are baptized in the church as soon after birth as is convenient. Each infant has two or three sponsors who do not seem to have any definite obligations or special relationship to the child as it grows up. The best liked, most competent people, as well as those who are thought to be "the most religious," are asked to be sponsors again and again. A check of the mission records shows that during the past fifteen years, about a dozen individuals have been sponsors at baptisms most of the time.

The Bishop of Alaska makes one visit to the village each year, usually in March, for the purpose of confirming those young people who have been prepared by a series of classes held by the missionary. These classes, which are held once or twice a week beginning before Christmas, are attended by children who have reached their twelfth birthday. Confirmation, though an extremely important event for the young people involved, is not marked by any family or community observance. All young people are proud of becoming full members of the Church, a fact symbolized by receiving their crosses from the bishop and by being able to partake of Holy Communion. Their families are proud of them on this occasion even though there is no celebration or other observance connected with it.

The services held on Sunday evenings in the parish hall are of particular interest because they are not a part of the regular Episcopal Church observances and are a relatively recent innovation in the village, having been started about twenty years ago. These services were originally for the purpose of discussing the morning's sermon, and that still is an important aspect of the procedure. The service is presided over by a member of the church council who delivers a short sermon, usually stressing some aspect of the morning's sermon, and reads appropriate texts from the Bible. A number of hymns are always sung by those present. The services are well attended by young people, who come mainly because they like to have a chance to sing their favorite hymns. Anyone attending the service may speak if he wishes, and several usually take advantage of this at each service, reading passages from the Bible or delivering short sermons. The hymns sung during this service do not come from the standard Episcopal hymn book, which is used at Sunday morning and Wednesday evening services, but rather from a book with predominantly more emotional and evangelical hymns.

The Sunday evening services are conducted entirely in Eskimo although the priest, who speaks only English, is present. He usually says a prayer at the beginning and end of the service but his role is otherwise largely inactive.

Some people in the village never attend the Sunday evening services because they feel that these meetings are often used for finger-pointing at the behavior of certain individuals in the village. Personal antagonisms occasionally have flared into the open through remarks made at the Sunday evening service.

The evening service on Sunday, differing as it does from the regular Episcopal services, may represent an attempt on the part of the people to interject individual participation and individual religious experiences, so typical of aboriginal beliefs and ceremonies, into the formal type of Christianity that they have accepted. Many Point Hope people have friends and relatives in Kotzebue who are members of the local Evangelical Friends Church. The beliefs and practices of this group infiltrated Point Hope to a certain extent and may also be reflected in the Sunday evening services.

Outside influence on the Point Hopers' religious attitudes are observable in still other aspects of their religious life. The more or less submerged opposition to the weekly films is probably due to the influence of the Evangelical Friends and other sect churches in Kotzebue. Although there is no overt objection to the motion pictures there are some people who do not approve and never attend. One woman told the missionary that when she has enough money to go to a show, she gives it to the Church. Although this woman is a strong Episcopalian, it is suggestive that one of her daughters in Kotzebue belongs to the Evangelical Friends Church.

There is a very strong feeling that there should be no dancing on Sunday, and Saturday night dances are usually stopped promptly at midnight. The Episcopal Church has never made any point of this, although there is some indication that one of the missionaries in the past may have objected because it kept people away from church. However, this was a long time ago and never has been stressed by subsequent missionaries. All the sect churches in Kotzebue consider dancing to be sinful and their influence in Point Hope seems clear. However, dancing, both Eskimo and American, is one of the favorite recreations of the Point Hopers and there seems little chance that it will ever be entirely eliminated, especially since the Wednesday evening dances are officially sponsored by the mission.

It is the custom in the village for everyone to give up something during Lent and the mission stresses this very strongly. The sacrifices made range from dancing, which is given up by everyone, no dances being held during this period, to films, various foods, tea, coffee, and games. During Lent, the Wednesday evening services are transferred from the parish hall to the church and the games and dances are eliminated. Presumably, people also make daily money contributions to "mite boxes" that are distributed by the mission to every family in the village. Although Lent is observed by nearly everyone, there are some people who feel that the restrictions should be even stronger. They object to motion pictures or any kind of public entertainment. At one of the Sunday evening services while I was in the village, a man delivered a tirade against the showing of films during Lent, contending that it was divine retribution that caused the school's projector to be broken at that particular time. Again outside influence is indicated since there is nothing in Episcopal Church practice that prohibits any particular activity during Lent.

An unusual situation that developed while I was at Point Hope afforded an opportunity to observe the attitude of the people toward their church and the extent to which it is woven into the social fabric. A female missionary of the Pentecostal Church, who arrived in the village without any advance notice, declared her intention of staying at least a year. She was able to find a place to live without any difficulty and obtained permission to use the National Guard building for services. People were considerably impressed by her statement that God had told her to come to Point Hope. The initial attitude was one of surprise. Everyone was curious but no one was particularly excited or upset. There was even some hopeful speculation that she might build a church in the village, thus providing local employment opportunities.

The Pentecostal missionary held no more than four or five services because, when cold weather came, she was unable to keep the National Guard building heated and had no money to hire assistance. Her services were fairly well attended, but most of those present seemed to be there out of curiosity or for entertainment. Many people were impressed by her flamboyant manner of preaching but were embarrassed and made highly uncomfortable by requests for personal testimonials.

Because of the presence of only one church in the village for over sixty years, the people are not used to looking at religion from a comparative standpoint. After the arrival of the Pentecostal missionary, people began asking questions about the belief of the sect, particularly with regard to its attitudes concerning smoking, dancing, card playing, and motion pictures. One man assured me that since the Pentecostals believed all these activities to be sinful, there was no danger that anyone in the village would become a member. Several individuals told me that they often thought about their friends in Kotzebue, Noatak, and Kivalina who belong to the Evangelical Friends Church and other sect groups and who had to give up smoking, dancing, card playing, and films. "They don't have any fun any more."

After remaining in the village about five months, the Pentecostal missionary was forced to leave, mostly because of lack of funds plus an inability to get along by herself in a rigorous environment. People were kind to her and even lent her money, but the problems of living alone in a village on the Arctic coast during the winter were too much for her. The type of religion she represented, one that appeals strongly to the emotions, might originally have had more attraction for the Eskimos than the more formal procedures of the Episcopal Church. However, it is now, for the most part, repellent to them. Many of them have attended the Pentecostal and Evangelical Friends services in Kotzebue and have heard evangelists on the radio. In the past, members of the Kotzebue Evangelical Friends Church have come to Point Hope to visit relatives and have attempted a certain amount of proselytizing. However, this has never been carried out extensively or with organization and has not been successful.

Point Hope people say that when they first heard about Christianity they liked and accepted it partly because it relieved their worries about shamans and partly because they liked the description of heaven.[11] Today, everyone in the community is baptized and, theoretically, a member of the Church in good standing. The missionary estimates that 50 per cent of the men in the village regularly attend church; this appears to be correct. It seemed to me that nearly everyone attended church at least half the time. Women attend more regularly than men, but that is because some men hunt or do other work on Sunday. Many people in the village feel that it is wrong to hunt or work on Sunday, but a sizable number of men, particularly those who are heavily oriented toward a subsistence economy, attend church only if the weather is unfavorable for hunting.

The Church is definitely a working part of the village and fully integrated into community life in a variety of ways. When an individual feels resentment against all others in the village, he finds that about the only action he can take to show his indignation or disapproval is to stop attending church; he boycotts the one socially approved activity in which nearly all the community takes part. Thus, the small faction of nonchurchgoers are usually people who have nothing against the Church, and who probably consider themselves religious and good Christians, but rather have something against those individuals who do attend church regularly. This does not mean, of course, that there are not those in the village who are rather lukewarm about going to church merely because they are not particularly interested or do not want to be bothered. However, these individuals are apt to be lukewarm about churchgoing and not religion itself.

The role of the missionary in the village, in many ways, is a rather difficult one. He must maintain friendly relations with everyone and yet avoid close friendships with specific individuals. If he is more closely associated with certain people than with others, the general suspicion arises that the favored individuals obtain more benefit from the mission or are the recipients of greater divine favor. Since the mission distributes a certain amount of largesse in the form of temporary employment, the missionary must be cautious. Some people report rumors concerning fellow villagers to the missionary or foster involvement with one faction or another because they enjoy the fuss that is created. On the other hand, several villagers told me that in the past missionaries have always tried to pry into the affairs of the people. It is true that

---

[11]Spencer, 1959, p. 381, makes a similar statement about the success of the mission at Point Barrow, Alaska.

there have been frequent and bitter conflicts with missionaries in the past and it is a tribute to the Point Hopers that the intensity of their religious feeling has not been affected by them.

Men who seldom attend church insist on wearing the crosses that were given them at confirmation, when they fall ill. Individuals who are admittedly bored by the church services because of failure to understand the rather complex language of the Episcopal ritual are worried at the thought of a person not being baptized or confirmed. In cases of serious illness, members of the family are always eager to have the missionary conduct a service of the Holy Communion at the bedside of the sick person. It seems that while some people are relatively indifferent to religious ritual, true skepticism and disbelief are nonexistent.

The church council, composed entirely of older men, seems to form a sort of inner circle from which many of the younger men consider themselves to be excluded. This is doubtless one of the reasons why many of the more educated younger men do not take an active part in church activities. Some individuals in this group object to having the sermons translated into Eskimo. Those with a good command of English find that translation interferes with their comprehension, and also that it is distracting to have attention called to the mistakes of the translator. Many of the younger people who speak and understand English feel that they should be given priority with regard to the services. However, the majority of the villagers decidedly disagree.

There can be no doubt that homogeneity in religious faith is an important factor in creating solidarity and serves as a unifying force in the village. Point Hope lacks the religious factionalism that characterizes many Alaskan villages and the people, united as they are by their membership in the single church, are provided with ideal patterns of behavior that are quite meaningful. In the village, ideal behavior patterns have always involved cooperation, helpfulness, loyalty, and the like, and the teachings of the Church tend to reinforce these. A person who is leading a Christian life is, ideally, doing no more than is expected of him. The fact that many people's lives are far from the ideal does not lessen the validity of the concept.

Surviving Attitudes toward Old Beliefs

Sixty years of Christian teaching have all but obliterated the body of aboriginal religious and other supernatural beliefs that helped the precontact Point Hoper to relate to his natural surroundings and solve some of the problems presented by a difficult environment. The last ceremonial structure disappeared more than forty years ago and the traditionally powerful shamans are but a memory even to the oldest inhabitants.

Many villagers have vague ideas about the hunting songs that were an important part of every man's hunting equipment fifty or sixty years ago. These songs, which a man usually inherited from his namesake, were jealously guarded; some men hummed them very quietly to themselves before they left home each morning to hunt on the ice (Rainey, 1947, p. 254). Some of the oldest men in the village are referred to as still knowing these songs, and stories are told about songs owned by specific individuals still living that could save the lives of people lost on the ice, stop the flight of a wounded polar bear, and assure safety and successful hunting in numerous ways.

Although hunting songs are no longer a reality to Point Hopers, their power is strongly believed in, mostly, it would seem, because it is almost inconceivable to present-day Eskimos that their predecessors could have hunted successfully without the use of rifles. They feel that something extra must have been necessary and that the songs were every bit as essential as the harpoons and lances.

Faith in the value of the old-time hunting songs is indicative of a certain aspect of modern Point Hope attitudes. Belief in the power of songs and shamans is not inconsistent with a modern, forward-looking approach to village problems. Old beliefs are not ridiculed, but rather respected; they were fine in the old days, but are not for the present. Point Hopers noticeably lack a sense of history in this context, and it may be for this reason that the past and the present can be reconciled with so little difficulty.

11

CONCLUSIONS:
THE VILLAGE
OF TOMORROW

IT IS MY INTENTION in this concluding chapter to discuss the questions that served as a guide for the research and to present conclusions based on the actual findings. A number of questions suggested themselves before the field work was undertaken, and served as a guide and orientation for the research and analysis. These questions can be grouped as follows:

The Work Round and Technology

1. Has the continued importance of the basic subsistence activities in a northern Alaskan coastal village acted as a stabilizing influence in village life?
2. In spite of new techniques and equipment, has the perpetuation of the old cycle of hunting activities helped people to identify with their culture and community?
3. Since there has been a gradual shift to a money economy in order to satisfy wants created through many years of contact with American and European culture, what has been the effect on community life of increased employment outside the village?
4. Will individuals who become adapted to a money economy be unable to combine it with aboriginal subsistence activities and leave the village?
5. What effect have changes in technology as a result of contact had on techniques of subsistence and the mechanics of daily living?
6. In what way have the Eskimos approached the new technology and what effect has it had on the former close relationship between craftsmanship and utility?

Social Structure

1. Has intensive contact brought about a demand for English-

speaking individuals for labor and other services within the village
and for employment outside the village?

2. What effect on the social order can be noted as a result of
the introduction of old-age benefits for individuals over sixty-five?

3. Have these changes, along with the permanent residence of
teachers and missionaries in a village, acted as an effective chal-
lenge to the community leadership of the family head whose importance was uppermost at the time when the powerful extended
families were the most important element of the village social
structure?

4. Are the prerequisites for leadership in an Eskimo village of
today different than they were under aboriginal conditions?

5. Has the changing social structure tended to rob the Eskimos
of all their old social identification and status while, in exchange,
allowing them to receive only partial acceptance in white social
organizations?

6. Since a new type of community organization has been introduced to compensate for the changed social structure, to what
extent does a village possess a common body of law that is appropriate to the new culture?

7. Is the new community organization genuinely operative and
not just a formal structure with no relationship to the realities of
village life?

The Individual

1. Having been exposed to conflicting influences over a long period of time, will the individual strive to associate himself with
indigenous attitudes in order to maintain his culture identity, and
be evasive when confronted with an alien idea from outside his
own culture?

2. If the individual has been able, in many instances, to continue
certain aboriginal complexes, particularly those associated with
subsistence activities, will skill in performing these techniques
give him a superior prestige position in those particular aspects
of the existing culture pattern?

3. Since the religion of the Eskimos in northwest Alaska has been
actively suppressed by missionaries for more than fifty years, is
the old religion completely obliterated, or does much of it still
remain, but kept from the view of the missionaries?

4. If Christianity has been totally accepted does it adequately fill
the religious needs of the people, or has there been a loss of ritual,

particularly with regard to the recognition of the various phases of an individual's life?

The following discussion is based on the material contained in the study and results from the questions listed above which, as previously mentioned, served as the problem orientation for the field work. The numbered comments correspond to the numbered questions and related questions are discussed together.

The Work Round and Technology

1, 2. A study of the seasonal cycle of subsistence activities at Point Hope has shown that in spite of new equipment and a few new techniques, the basic pattern remains much the same as it was in the precontact period. The people are still essentially sea-mammal hunters and many aspects of their life in the village are related to this fact. The village has been successful in maintaining a stable population while other subsistence-centered villages are disintegrating, largely because of this attitude toward the economy. In spite of interests outside the village, local men maintain their primary interest in the yearly round of hunting enterprises, and regulate their other activities so as not to interfere with them. Hunting can be said to be the major orientation of the village and the villagers are proud that they inhabit one of the best hunting locations on the Arctic coast.

3, 4. In spite of the continued significance of the old cycle of subsistence activities, nearly every Point Hoper is involved with two separate and simultaneous economic systems, a money economy and a subsistence economy. The growth of communications and increased contacts with the outside world has done much to spread the American mass culture to Point Hope. Everyone in the village is influenced by the radio, magazines, and the movies. The wants that have thus been created can be satisfied only by the possession of a money income. Since the end of the second world war, employment opportunities in Alaska have increased because of the large amount of military construction, and the fact that most of it takes place during the summer months has made it possible for Point Hope men to fit outside employment into their seasonal cycle at a time when there is little going on in the village. Thus individuals can become adapted to a money economy and still combine it with aboriginal subsistence activities. For this reason, there has been no complete shift to a money economy, and consequently no depopulation of the village in favor of the large urban centers. However, as more and more young people leave the village to complete their education and become more oriented toward a money economy, it is possible that they will become correspondingly disoriented from village subsistence activities and will seek economic opportunities away from the village.

5, 6. Perhaps the most obvious aspects of change in Point Hope culture pertain to technology and have resulted in the almost complete abandonment of the traditional Eskimo material culture. Nearly all tools and weapons now in use in the village are manufactured rather than homemade and must be purchased with cash. Even the few that are made in the village (sleds, dog harnesses, boats) require in their manufacture some material that must be purchased. Aboriginal methods and concepts have been replaced rapidly by the most recent twentieth century methods and concepts, and the people of Point Hope, far from regarding such change suspiciously, have been quick to recognize the advantages of efficient new techniques and instruments. There has been an almost complete Americanization of household and personal equipment—furniture, cooking utensils, flashlights, radios, and the like. Such changes, together with those involving the subsistence economy, have been accepted despite the fact that in some cases they involve excessive expense and their procurement works a hardship on the individuals involved. Although formerly the relationship between craftsmanship and utility was close, the changes in material culture do not seem to be in conflict, either functionally or symbolically, with other firmly established and unchanging norms of village behavior. Instead, individuals within the existing culture marvel at the way their predecessors were able to exist satisfactorily without the new methods and techniques that they take for granted today.

Social Structure

1. Intensive contact and the changing economy have definitely brought about a demand for English-speaking individuals for labor and other services, both within the village and for employment outside the village. It has been noted that the village council is being made up increasingly of individuals who have an adequate command of English and are in a position to act as effective spokesmen for the village in relations with teachers, missionaries, and organizations outside the village. There also seems to be a direct relationship between an adequate command of English and skilled or semiskilled high-paying summer construction jobs. Those who

speak little or no English are usually unable to find work except in relatively low-paying unskilled jobs where there is a minimum of verbal contact with whites. Everyone in the village realizes the importance of being able to speak good English.

2. The relatively recent introduction of old-age benefits for individuals over sixty five has not had a profound effect on the social order. In the aboriginal culture, old people were feared for their supernatural powers and every effort was made to appease and placate them. However, aside from certain aspects of ceremonial life, they did not exert the great influence in community affairs that has been noted for primitive peoples in other parts of the world. Effective social control rested, and still rests to a large extent, in the active hunters who are family heads. Old people today may make important contributions to the family in an economic sense because of old-age benefits, but this has not increased or decreased their prestige or their position in the social order.

3, 4. The decline and virtual disappearance of the large extended families at Point Hope has, more than anything else, served to reduce the importance of the family head in the village social structure. In spite of this, leadership patterns do not seem to have undergone as great a change as might be expected. The most important men in the village are still the good hunters and whaling captains. If these individuals also happen to be strongly associated with the Church, it does them no harm. However, being strongly associated with the Church is not enough in itself to insure a position of leadership. The most obvious village leader is the council president, and in recent years the tendency has been to elect an individual who speaks good English and is an adequate spokesman for the village in contacts with the outside world. The less obvious aspects of leadership are seen in day-to-day activities; under these circumstances, the successful hunters and whaling captains function as leaders. If these individuals are also well adjusted to a money economy it enhances their position in the eyes of the villagers, and their prestige is correspondingly increased. Although leadership qualities remain much the same as in the past, the individuals who possess them are no longer the heads of large extended families and their influence is thus correspondingly decreased.

5. Although the changing social structure has, to a certain extent, destroyed some of the social identification and status that was formerly enjoyed, the villagers do not seem to be particularly conscious of receiving only partial acceptance in white social organization. Admittedly, this is something that might cause more

of a problem were the day-to-day contacts with whites more intensive than they are. Certainly such a problem exists in the larger
urban centers such as Nome, Kotzebue, and Fairbanks. Most Point
Hope men have seen that they can compete satisfactorily with white
men from an economic standpoint if given the chance. They belong
to the same unions, are hired for the same jobs, and work together
successfully with whites. Since they are in contact with whites
only during the summer they have few opportunities to experience
the results of racial prejudice. It is my impression that few individuals in the village are oriented in any way toward the outside
world, except with regard to employment. Their own problems and
position in the village occupy a place uppermost in their thoughts
and they are not concerned, overtly at least, with their relationships to an essentially alien social structure. A few persons, however, appear to feel strongly the fact that they are caught between
two cultures; their own, with which they are thoroughly familiar but
to which complete return is neither possible nor desirable, and
American culture, the many ramifications of which are confusing
to their minds. Individuals in this category are apt to be those who
are unsuccessful at typical Eskimo pursuits or who have become
successful in the village by means of activities that are essentially
non-Eskimo, such as postmaster, storekeeper, and the like.

    6, 7. The Indian Reorganization Act resulted in the introduction
of the village council system to many Alaskan villages. This system has been notably unsuccessful in many of these villages because it is merely a formal structure and has no meaning in village life and no power in terms of the new culture. In many cases,
village councils have become nothing more than stages on which
village factionalism is played or, at best, representative of only
a small minority in the village. At Point Hope, the village council
is probably more genuinely operative than in most other villages.
However, it lacks the means for enforcing its decisions and appears to be only moderately successful as a liaison between the
village and outside law-enforcement agencies. The general absence in the old days of any group or organization having disciplinary powers has made it difficult for the council to become
established as a functioning regulatory group appropriate to the
new culture. The effectiveness of the council depends heavily on the
prestige and social status of its members, and the system of elections has generally assured that individuals properly qualified have
held the positions. In this way the villagers express, in a formal
way, a factor of village influence and control that is inherent in
Eskimo culture. The fact that new types of leadership are making

their appearance in the village is indicative of culture change but not a change in basic values.

The Individual

1, 2. The individual does not find it necessary to strive to associate himself with indigenous attitudes for the purpose of maintaining his cultural identity. There are still many aspects of Point Hope life that allow the individual naturally to identify himself with the Eskimo way of life. This is particularly true with regard to subsistence activities, and particularly hunting on the ice, an activity in which a white man cannot hope to take part without the assistance and instruction of Eskimos. There are many techniques associated with Eskimo culture that still allow an individual to maintain a superior prestige position within the existing culture pattern, greatly changed though it may be.

However, a few individuals find that this is not adequate and give considerable thought to the position of the Eskimo in the over-all scheme of things. These are the individuals who have difficulty in reconciling the apparent inventiveness and rapid development associated with American culture with the traditional aspects of Eskimo culture, and in accepting the fact that the latter has become subordinate to the former. For them the Eskimo way seems backward and uninventive and this feeling, which is incompatible with cultural identification, makes adjustments difficult for these individuals.

3, 4. The people of Point Hope have been exposed to Christianity for more than sixty years. Over this long period of time, with a minimum of strife, the old religion appears to have been completely obliterated and Christianity totally accepted. Some individuals are more religiously oriented than others, but it appears that the village as a whole is considerably more guided by Christian teachings and influenced by Christian ritual than most communities or congregations of comparable size in the rest of the United States. The ritual aspects of the Episcopalian services are particularly pleasing to the villagers and were doubtless readily accepted and understood by a people whose old religion depended much upon ritual for its effect.

In spite of the abundance of ritual in the Episcopal Church service and its total acceptance by the people, it is very likely that the villagers have suffered a loss of ritual particularly with regard to celebrating the various phases of an individual's life. While the preparation for taking first communion has considerable meaning

to the average Point Hoper, there no longer exists a system of
community recognition for the first emergence as a contributing
member of the family and community. Ceremonies celebrating the
first killing of various types of animals have been reduced to the
point where they no longer have meaning from the standpoint of
the whole community. The advent of a new hunter or a new wage
earner is relatively unrecognized by the group even though individual families may make much of it. Whether or not this ritual
loss is significant, the fact remains that a force binding the community together and stressing the interdependence of its members
has been weakened.

The Village of Tomorrow

There are certain aspects of Point Hope life that point to factors that may be significant in the future, granted that any great
changes will come from outside the village and will involve situations over which the villagers have little or no control.

The village is fortunate in its geographical location. The excellence of the sea hunting is at least partly responsible for the
retention of the aboriginal cycle of subsistence activities, and has
also been the major factor in population stability. There is still
much to bind the Point Hoper to his village and it is likely that this
situation will continue for some time in the future. However, as is
the case with everyone living in Alaska, the future of the village
depends on government construction plans and other factors in the
present inflated economic situation in the new state. If the time
should come when summer employment away from the village no
longer satisfies new-felt needs, a movement of people from the
village to the urban centers can be expected.

Another question mark of the future concerns those young individuals who are leaving the village to complete their education
and the unpredictability of their return. If they do return they will
not be closely tied to the subsistence pattern of the village. Having
learned trades at school, they would presumably find little in village life to attract them; but if the economic outlook in Alaska
should change, they might be forced to return.

The situation of the Point Hopers today is fairly good. They have
enough to eat except occasionally during the autumn months. From
a nutritional point of view the diet is not well balanced but malnu-
trition is practically unknown. Sanitary conditions and general village health are fair but there is much room for improvement.
Present health programs in the area do not stress education. As

a result, the people are largely ignorant concerning hygiene and health preservation, nor do they fully understand the relationship between uncleanliness and disease. Public health improvement in the village will be a large task, and large amounts of money spent for the purpose will not be profitable until an effective program of health education is instituted.

Regarding family life, an important point should be made. Most of the economic and social situations are still based on the family rather than on the individual. Hunting is essentially a family activity, success or failure depending upon the extent to which the needs of the family are satisfied. In principle, if not always in practice, every member does his or her best to increase the income and productivity of the family. There is no sharp differentiation; if one member works harder, he does not get more; if another is lazy and does not work, he does not get less. In other words, the totality of subsistence activities is a communal affair from the family standpoint. The annual spring whale hunt stresses the communal aspect of hunting as it involves everyone in the village. The strength of family attachments becomes weakened when one member works for money outside the village. A married man usually sends such earnings to his wife and children, but an unmarried man often does not feel obligated to turn over even a small portion of his wages to his family.

In summary, the family structure of Point Hope, although considerably modified from aboriginal times, is still a strong aspect of communal solidarity. As long as the village retains its present economic structure, this situation is likely to continue and the village will be strengthened accordingly.

The village organization at Point Hope today is essentially forward looking. Elected village officials have embarked on a program of civic improvements and appear eager to achieve for the village as high a standard of living as possible, a point of view which is, understandably, enthusiastically supported by the great majority of the villagers. There are a minimum of village factions and those that exist are based on a conflict of personality rather than of ideas. There is no strong group in favor of the past; people talk about "the good old days," but no one wants to return to them. The community has its collective eye on the future and is eager to make the best of the many opportunities that have come its way in the postwar world. This strong sense of village solidarity is the best protection against an uncertain future.

BIBLIOGRAPHY

Aldrich, H. L.
  1889 *Arctic Alaska and Siberia, or, Eight Months with the Arctic Whalemen.* Chicago: Rand, McNally and Co.
Anderson, H. D., and Eells, W. C.
  1935 *Alaska Natives: A Survey of Their Sociological and Educational Status.* Stanford, California: Stanford University Press.
Beechey, F. W.
  1831 *Narrative of a Voyage to the Pacific and Beering's Strait, 1825-1828.* 2 vols. London: H. Colburn and R. Bentley.
Birket-Smith, K.
  1953 "The Chugach Eskimo," *Etnografisk Raekke* (Copenhagen: Nationalmuseets Skrifter), Vol. VI.
Collier, A. J.
  1906 *Geology and Coal Resources of the Cape Lisbourne Region.* Bulletin of the U.S. Geological Survey, No. 278.
Cook, J. A.
  1926 *Pursuing the Whale: A Quarter Century of Whaling in the Arctic.* New York: Houghton Mifflin Co.
Driggs, J. B.
  1903 "A Busy Year at Point Hope," *Spirit of Missions* (New York), Vol. LXVIII, No. 11.
Giddings, J. L., Jr.
  1952a *The Arctic Woodland Culture of the Kobuk River.* Museum Monographs, University Museum. Philadelphia, University of Pennsylvania.
  1952b "Observations on the 'Eskimo Type' of Kinship and Social Structure," *Anthropological Papers of the University of Alaska*, I, No. 1, 5-10.
  1956 *Forest Eskimos: An Ethnographic Sketch of Kobuk River*

People in the 1880's. University Museum, The University
Museum Bulletin. Philadelphia, University of Pennsylvania.

Goodman, F. W.
1940   "The Jubilee of St. Thomas Mission," *The Alaska Church-
man,* Vol. XXXV, No. 3.

Hadwen, S., and Palmer, L. J.
1922   *Reindeer in Alaska.* U. S. Department of Agriculture, Bulletin No. 1089.

Healy, M. A.
1889   *Report of the Cruise of the Revenue Marine Steamer* Corwin *in the Arctic Ocean in the Year 1884.* Washington,
D. C.: U. S. Government Printing Office.

Hooper, C. L.
1881   *Report of the Cruise of the U. S. Revenue Steamer* Corwin *in the Arctic Ocean, November 1, 1880.* Washington,
D. C.: U. S. Government Printing Office.

Hughes, C. C.
1958   "An Eskimo Deviant from the Eskimo Type of Social Organization," *American Anthropologist* (Menasha, Wiscon-
sin), LX, No. 6, 1140-47.
1960   *An Eskimo Village in the Modern World.* Ithaca, New
York: Cornell University Press.

Jackson, S.
1904   *Fourteenth Annual Report on Introduction of Domestic
Reindeer into Alaska, 1904,* in Annual Report of the Education Bureau (58th Cong., 3d sess.; S. Doc. 61, in v.
2; 4764). Washington, D. C.: U. S. Government Printing
Office.

Kindle, E. M.
1909   "Notes on the Point Hope Spit, Alaska," *Journal of Geology,* XVII, 178-89.

Lantis, M.
1946   "The Social Culture of the Nunivak Eskimo," *Transactions
of the American Philosophical Society* (Philadelphia), Vol.
XXXV, No. 3.
1952a   "Eskimo Herdsmen: Introduction of Reindeer Herding to
the Natives of Alaska," *Human Problems and Technologi-
cal Change,* Chap. 8. New York: Russell Sage Foundation.
1952b   "Present Status of the Alaskan Eskimos," *Science in
Alaska: Selected Papers of the Alaskan Science Confer-
ence of the National Academy of Sciences, National Re-*

search Council. Washington, D. C. : The Arctic Institute of North America.
1954   "Problems of Ecology in the North American Arctic," *Arctic* (Ottawa), Vol. VII, Nos. 3 and 4.
1960   *Eskimo Childhood and Interpersonal Relationships*. Seattle: University of Washington Press.

Larsen, H. , and Rainey, F. G.
1948   "Ipiutak and the Arctic Whale Hunting Culture," *Anthropological Papers of the American Museum of Natural History* (New York), Vol. XLII.

Lavrischeff, T. I.
1935   History of Education in Alaska. Unpublished Ph. D. thesis, Department of Education, University of California.

Murdoch, J.
1892   "The Ethnological Results of the Point Barrow Expedition," *Ninth Annual Report of the Bureau of Ethnology* (1887-88), pp. 3-441. Washington, D. C. : U. S. Government Printing Office.

Murdock, G. P.
1949   *Social Structure*. New York: The Macmillan Company.

Nelson, E. W.
1899   "The Eskimo about Bering Strait," *Eighteenth Annual Report of the Bureau of American Ethnology* (1896-97), pp. 3-518. Washington, D. C. : U. S. Government Printing Office.

Rabot, C.
1914   "The Whale Fisheries of the World," *Annual Report of the Smithsonian Institution, 1913* (Washington, D. C.).

Rainey, F. G.
1947   "The Whale Hunters of Tigara," *Anthropological Papers of the American Museum of Natural History* (New York), Vol. XLI, Part II.

Rasmussen, K.
1927   *Across Arctic America: Narrative of the Fifth Thule Expedition*. New York and London: G. P. Putnam's Sons.

Ray, P. H.
1885   "Ethnographical Sketch of the Natives of Point Barrow," *Report of the International Expedition to Point Barrow*. Washington, D. C. : U. S. Government Printing Office.

Spencer, R. F.
1959   *The North Alaskan Eskimo: A Study in Ecology and Society*. Smithsonian Institution, Bureau of American Eth-

nology, Bulletin No. 171. Washington, D. C.: U. S. Government Printing Office.

Stuck, H.
1920 *The Alaskan Missions of the Episcopal Church*. New York: Domestic and Foreign Missionary Society.

Tikhmenev, P.
1863 *The Historical Review of Formation of the Russian American Company and Its Activity up to the Present Time*. 2 parts. Translated by D. Krenov, 1940. Seattle: Work Projects Administration, 1939-40.

Tower, W. S.
1907 *A History of the American Whale Fishery*. (Publications of the University of Pennsylvania, Series in Political Economy and Public Law.) Philadelphia.

U. S. Census Bureau
1884 "Report on the Population, Industries, and Resources of Alaska," *10th Census*. Washington, D. C.: U. S. Government Printing Office.
1893 "Report on the Population and Resources of Alaska," *11th Census*. Washington, D. C.: U. S. Government Printing Office.

U. S. Revenue Service
1899 *Report of the Cruise of the U. S. Revenue-Cutter* Bear *and the Overland Expedition for the Relief of the Whalers in the Arctic Ocean from November 27, 1897 to September 18, 1898*. Washington, D. C.: U. S. Government Printing Office.

VanStone, J. W.
1958a "The Autobiography of an Alaskan Eskimo," *Arctic* (Ottawa), X, No. 4, 195-210.
1958b "Commercial Whaling in the Arctic Ocean," *Pacific Northwest Quarterly*, XLIX, No. 1, 1-10.
1958c "An Eskimo Community and the Outside World," *Anthropological Papers of the University of Alaska*, VII, No. 1, 27-38.
1960 "A Successful Combination of Subsistence and Wage Economies on the Village Level," *Economic Development and Cultural Change* (Chicago), VIII, No. 2, 174-91.

Wells, R.
1890 *English-Eskimo and Eskimo-English Vocabularies*. U. S. Bureau of Education Circular of Information No. 2.

PUBLICATIONS OF THE AMERICAN ETHNOLOGICAL SOCIETY

Law and Status among the Kiowa Indians. Jane Richardson. (Monograph I) 1940. 142 pages, bibliography. Out of print

Rank and Warfare among the Plains Indians. Bernard Mishkin. (Monograph III) 1940. 73 pages, bibliography. Out of print

Disease, Religion and Society in the Fiji Islands. Dorothy M. Spencer. (Monograph II) 1941. 92 pages, chart. Out of print

An Analysis of Inca Militarism. Joseph Bram. (Monograph IV) 1941. 93 pages, bibliography. Out of print

A Primitive Mexican Economy. George M. Foster. (Monograph V) 1942. 123 pages, plates, maps, bibliography. Out of print

The Effects of White Contact upon Blackfoot Culture, with Special Reference to the Role of the Fur Trade. Oscar Lewis. (Monograph VI) 1942. 79 pages, maps, bibliography. Out of print

Arapesh. R. F. Fortune. (Publication XIX) 1942. 243 pages. $5.00

Prayer: The Compulsive Word. Gladys A. Reichard. (Monograph VII) 1944. 121 pages, figures, bibliography. Out of print

Changing Configurations in the Social Organization of a Blackfoot Tribe during the Reserve Period (The Blood of Alberta, Canada). Esther S. Goldfrank. (Monograph VIII) 1945. 81 pages, plates, bibliography. (Bound with IX). Out of print

Observations on Northern Blackfoot Kinship. L. M. Hanks, Jr., and Jane Richardson. (Monograph IX) 1945. 37 pages, figures. (Bound with VIII). Out of print

Map of North American Indian Languages. Compiled and drawn by C. F. Voegelin and E. W. Voegelin. (Publication XX) 1945. Wall size, color. Out of print

The Influence of Islam on a Sudanese Religion. Joseph Greenberg. (Monograph X) 1946. 83 pages, figures, map, bibliography. Out of print

Alaskan Eskimo Ceremonialism. Margaret Lantis. (Monograph XI) 1947. 143 pages, maps, bibliography. Out of print

Economics of the Mount Hagen Tribes, New Guinea. Abraham L. Gitlow. (Monograph XII) 1947. 122 pages, plates, figures, maps, bibliography. Out of print

Ceremonial Patterns in the Greater Southwest. Ruth M. Underhill (Monograph XIII) 1948. 74 pages, bibliography, index. (Bound with XIV)

Factionalism in Isleta Pueblo. David H. French. (Monograph XIV) 1948. 54 pages, bibliography. (Bound with XIII) $2.50

The Negro in Northern Brazil: A Study in Acculturation. Octavio da Costa Eduardo. (Monograph XV) 1948. 139 pages, map, bibliography. Out of print

Bali: Rangda and Barong. Jane Belo. (Monograph XVI) 1949. 71 pages, plates, figures, bibliography. $2.75

The Rubber-Ball Games of the Americas. Theodore Stern. (Monograph XVII) 1950. 129 pages, plate, maps, bibliography. Out of print

Fighting with Property: A Study of Kwakiutl Potlatching and Warfare 1792-1930. Helen Codere. With Tribal and Linguistic Map of Vancouver Island and Adjacent Territory, drawn and compiled by Vincent F. Kotschar. (Monograph XVIII) 1950. 143 pages, figures, maps, charts, bibliography. $3.00

The Cheyenne in Plains Indian Trade Relations 1795-1840. Joseph Jablow. (Monograph XIX) 1951. 110 pages, maps, bibliography, index. $2.50

The Tsimshian: Their Arts and Music. The Tsimshian and Their Neighbors, by Viola E. Garfield; Tsimshian Sculpture, by Paul S. Wingert; Tsimshian Songs, by Marius Barbeau. (Publication XVIII) 1951. 302 pages, plates, figures, maps, music, bibliography, index. $6.00

Navaho Grammar. Gladys A. Reichard. (Publication XXI) 1951. 407 pages, bibliography. $7.00

Buzios Island: A Caiçara Community in Southern Brazil. Emilio Willems in cooperation with Gioconda Mussolini. (Monograph XX) 1952. 124 pages, figures, maps, bibliography. $2.75

Chichicastenango: A Guatemalan Village. Ruth Bunzel. (Publication XXII) 1952. 464 pages, figures, bibliography. $7.00

Changing Military Patterns on the Great Plains (17th Century through Early 19th Century). Frank Raymond Secoy. (Monograph XXI) 1953. 120 pages, maps, bibliography. $2.75

Bali: Temple Festival. Jane Belo. (Monograph XXII) 1953. 78 pages, plates, chart, bibliography. $2.75

Hungarian and Vogul Mythology. Géza Róheim. With appendixes by John Lotz. (Monograph XXIII) 1954. 96 pages, map, bibliography. Out of print

The Trumaí Indians of Central Brazil. Robert F. Murphy and Buell Quain. (Monograph XXIV) 1955. 120 pages, plates, map, bibliography. $2.75

The Deeply Rooted: A Study of a Drents Community in the Netherlands. John Y. Keur and Dorothy L. Keur. (Monograph XXV) 1955. 208 pages, plates, maps, bibliography. Out of print

The Tlingit Indians: Results of a Trip to the Northwest Coast of America and the Bering Straits. Aurel Krause. Translated by Erna Gunther. 1956. 320 pages, plates, figures, map, bibliography, index. $4.50

Village and Plantation Life in Northeastern Brazil. Harry William Hutchinson. 1957. 209 pages, plates, maps, charts, bibliography, index. $3.50

Malaya. Norton Ginsburg and Chester F. Roberts, Jr. 1958. 546 pages, maps, charts, bibliography, index. $6.75

Social Stratification in Polynesia. Marshall D. Sahlins. 1958. 320 pages, figures, bibliography. $4.50

Status Terminology and the Social Structure of North American Indians. Munro S. Edmonson. 1958. 92 pages, charts, bibliography. $3.00

A Community in the Andes: Problems and Progress in Muquiyauyo. Richard N. Adams. 1959. 266 pages, maps, figures, bibliography, index. $4.75

Land and Polity in Tibet. Pedro Carrasco. 1959. 318 pages, maps, bibliography, index. $5.75

Eskimo Childhood and Interpersonal Relationships: Nunivak Biographies and Genealogies. Margaret Lantis. 1960. 232 pages, map, figures, charts, bibliography. $5.00

Carribbean Studies: A Symposium. Vera Rubin, ed. (2nd ed.), 1960. 124 pages, map, references, notes on contributors. $3.00

West Indian Family Structure. M. G. Smith. 1962. app. 256 pages, 100 pages of tables included. $6.00

Point Hope: An Eskimo Community in Transition. James W. VanStone. 1962. 163 pages, maps, illustrations, bibliography. $5.25

Papago Pottery. Bernard L. Fontana, William J. Robinson, Charles W. Cormack, and Ernest E. Leavitt, Jr. Maps, drawings, photographs. $5.75 (tent.)